# 365

## *activities*

## you and your baby will love

GYMBOREE PLAY & MUSIC

# 365

## activities

## you and your baby
## will love

author
**susan elisabeth davis**

consultant editors
**dr. roni cohen leiderman & dr. wendy masi**

illustrator
**christine coirault**

photographer
**aaron locke**

**BONNIER BOOKS**

# GYMBOREE. PLAY & MUSIC

This edition published by
Bonnier Books, Appledram Barns,
Birdham Road, Chichester, West Sussex PO20 7EQ, UK

**Gymboree Play & Music**
Chief Executive Officer **Matthew McCauley**
Vice President, Gymboree Play & Music **Jill Johnston**
Merchandise Manager **Dawn Sagorski**
Senior Programme Developer **Helene Silver Freda**

**Weldon Owen Inc.**
Chief Executive Officer **John Owen**
Chief Operating Officer & President **Terry Newell**
Chief Financial Officer **Christine E. Munson**
Vice President, Publisher **Roger Shaw**
Vice President, Creative Director **Gaye Allen**
Vice President, International Sales **Stuart Laurence**

Publisher **Rebecca Poole Forée**
Managing Editor **Jennifer Block Martin**
Project Editor **Maria Behan**
Contributing Editors **Elizabeth Dougherty,
Margaret Sabo Wills**
UK Adaptation **Grant Laing Partnership**
Copy Editor **Gail Nelson-Bonebrake**
Proofreader **Jacqueline K. Aaron**
Indexer **Ken DellaPenta**
Editorial Assistant **Lucie Parker**

Art Director **Lisa Milestone**
Production Director **Chris Hemesath**
Production Assistant **Meghan Hildebrand**

ISBN-13: 978-1-905825-16-5

Printed in China.

## a special note on safety

At Gymboree, we encourage parents to become active play partners with their children. As you enjoy these enriching activities with your baby, make safety your priority. While the risk of injury during any of these activities is low, take every precaution to ensure that your child is safe.

To reduce the risk of injury, please follow these guidelines: do not leave your child unattended, even for a brief moment, during any of the activities in this book; be particularly cautious when participating in the activities involving water because of the risk of drowning; ensure that your baby does not place in his or her mouth any small objects (even those depicted in the photographs and illustrations), as some may pose a choking hazard and could be fatal if ingested; make sure that writing and crafts materials are non-toxic and have been approved for use by children under three years of age.

Throughout this book, we have suggested guidelines to the age appropriateness of each activity; however, it is up to you to assess your own child's suitability for a particular activity before attempting it. Ability, balance, and dexterity vary considerably from child to child, even for children of the same age.

While we have made every effort to ensure that the information is accurate and reliable, and that the activities are safe and workable when an adult is properly supervising, we disclaim all liability for any unintended, unforeseen, or improper application of the recommendations and suggestions featured in this book.

# contents

six
months & up
173

nine
months & up
267

# Foreword

Tummy tickles, peekaboo games, silly songs, and bubble blowing: the many ways parents use play to connect with their infants are endless. Play is universal – and it's the natural way to interact with your baby. But play is much more than just fun and games. It's how babies learn about themselves, others, and everything around them.

Gymboree's *365 Activities You and Your Baby Will Love* provides you with an idea for each day of your newborn's pivotal first year. These play activities are designed not only to entertain your infant, but also to help him or her learn about the world, hone physical and mental skills, and grow closer to you. Many of the activities originated from Gymboree's ever-popular Play & Music Programmes. And to mirror your baby's major developmental milestones, the activities are divided into three-month age ranges, starting at birth and ending at 12 months.

Delight in your newborn's first year. The 365 days ahead are a journey that will bring more joy, fun, and fulfilment than you can imagine. Each day brings you opportunities to discover activities your baby will love and learn from – and we hope this book will be a great source of inspiration.

*Dr. Roni Cohen Leiderman*

*Dr. Wendy Masi*

# 0+
## birth & up

Newborn babies are fascinating creatures. Their senses are developing, they're highly attuned to you, and they're engaged in their very first experiences of the world. At this age, play has more to do with comfort, bonding, and trust than it does with lively interactive activities. You can help your baby develop her muscles and sensory abilities at this stage, too. Just take it slowly, and give her plenty of breaks to ensure that she doesn't become over-stimulated.

1

# soothe with heartbeats

Studies show that newborn babies are soothed by
the sound of a human heartbeat, which they grew
accustomed to hearing in the womb. Let your baby
experience this comforting sound often by lying with him
on your chest, skin to skin. Or sit in a chair and let his
head rest against the left side of your chest, which is the
side on which most mothers intuitively hold their babies
anyway. Notice how the sound and feel of your beating
heart can calm your newborn baby.

# 2

## talk often

Your baby is keenly attuned to the sound of your voice and to your facial expressions – she needs to be exposed to both to learn how to talk. Speak gently to soothe her, or talk quickly in an upbeat tone and with a range of facial expressions to make her eyes widen and her little head bobble with excitement.

# 3

## revel in his reflection

Babies are very aware of faces, especially those of other babies. Let your baby indulge in this fascination by gazing at himself in the mirror for a while. He won't know who's looking back at him until he is about 12 to 15 months old, but he's bound to like what he sees.

# 4

## take cues from your baby

The watchful eyes of a young baby are truly enchanting, in part because they are such obvious signs of intelligent, responsive life. But young babies are alert only for half an hour or so at a time and easily become over-stimulated when presented with too much activity.

How can you tell if she's had enough? Make sure you tune into the cues your baby's giving you. She may turn her head away, start to cry, or become sleepy. Respecting her need for space or for interaction will give her a chance to control how much stimulation she's taking in. As a result, she'll feel confident about her place in – and effect on – the world.

# 5

## lie under the trees

Together you and your newborn baby can watch the dance of light and shadow, feel the breeze upon your skin, and listen to the gentle *shhh shhh* of rustling leaves.

# 6

## take a walk

A walk in the great outdoors will quiet – and
fascinate – most babies, whether they're riding
in a pushchair or nestled close to your chest. And
fresh air can do wonders for new parents, too.

# 7

## tantalize with texture

Stroke large swatches of textured cloth such as velvet,
fake fur, corduroy, or satin across your baby's body.
As his grasping ability develops, he'll start to hold the
swatches himself and rub them between his fingers.
(Make sure the swatches are at least 15 x 15 cm, or
6 x 6 in, so they won't pose a choking hazard.)
At around six months, he may even choose one to
provide him comfort as he falls asleep at night.

# 8

## rise and shine

Greet your baby in the morning with this much-loved poem by Robert Louis Stevenson.

*A birdie with a yellow bill*
*Hopped upon my window sill.*
*Cocked his shining eye and said,*
*"Get up, get up, you sleepyhead!"*

# 9

## look out of the window

Give your baby time to gaze out of a window. The gentle sway of the curtains in the breeze, the flickering shadows, and the sights and sounds of passing birds will entrance her, as well as stimulate her vision and sharpen her ability to locate noises coming from different directions.

# 10

## dress alike

From the moment you bring your baby home, well-meaning observers will tell you how to dress your child. Often the recommendation will be to put more clothing on him. However, too much clothing can result in dangerous overheating. While newborn babies need to be kept warm because they can't regulate their own temperature, after the first month, a baby's body is able to conserve heat.

Here's a good rule of thumb: for newborn babies, put on one more layer of clothing than you're wearing. After the first month, your baby doesn't need to wear any more or less clothing than you do (unless you've built up a sweat from exercise or another activity).

# 11

"look me in the eyes...
Eye contact makes me feel
attached and teaches me
how to talk without words."

# 12

## play familiar tunes

Newborn babies perk up to music they heard in the womb – whether it was Bach, U2, or big sister's warbling rendition of "Rock-a-Bye Baby". Playing familiar music will stimulate your baby's mind and help her feel like her new world is safe and interesting.

# 13

## make funny noises

Your baby loves to hear you talk and laugh. You can help stimulate his auditory development – and get a good giggle going – by making all sorts of funny noises. Try squawking like a parrot, honking like a lorry hooter, or saying "hello, hello, hello!" in a squeaky voice. He'll be amused – and amazed – and someday will surprise you by initiating silly sounds himself.

# 14

## trace the tootsies

This light tickle game teaches about body parts.

*Round and round the baby's feet*
trace your fingers around your baby's feet

*The birdie says, "Tweet, tweet, tweet!"*
tap your fingers on her feet

*Round and round the baby's head*
trace your fingers around her head

*Now the birdie says, "It's time for bed!"*
kiss her forehead

# 15

## tickle, tickle, tickle

Tickling your newborn baby with a clean feather duster helps him feel where his body begins and ends. Keep "dusting" your baby, and by about three months of age he's likely to giggle every time you pull out that "toy".

# 16

## stretch out

Stretching your newborn baby's arms and legs helps her uncurl from her foetal position and become aware of her limbs. Gently pull her arms above her head, one at a time, then slowly pull her legs down, one at a time, until they're almost straight. Be sure to stop if your baby isn't enjoying the stretches.

# 17

## pat baby's back

When your baby is fractious, sleepy, or just needing a little physical contact, pat him gently on his back. This action helps him dispel wind, distracts him from too much stimulation in his environment, and simply reassures him that you're there.

# 18

## wear your wee one

You'll quickly realize that your baby's favourite place to be is right against your chest. Many babies, in fact, start fussing as soon as they are set down. Your infant's need for physical contact — and rhythmic motion — is natural; instinct tells her that she needs to be near someone to be safe. Satisfy her desire for contact by "wearing" her, in either a sling or a front carrier. An oft-cited study of mother-infant pairs found that six-week-old babies who were "worn" for at least three hours a day cried only half as much as those babies who were not. Carrying your infant also helps her develop the muscles required to sit, stand, and walk, because she is in a semi-upright or upright position, which naturally strengthens her neck and back muscles.

# 19

## flatter him

When your baby tries to imitate you, it shows that you're his first and most important teacher. So imagine how flattered he'll feel when you imitate his gentle coos, his sweet "ahhhhs", and his quirky, crooked smiles. It's a wonderful way to make him feel that he's someone special.

# 20

## start cycling lessons

Moving your baby's legs in a cycling motion helps her develop awareness of her tiny body. It also strengthens her abdominal muscles and introduces her to the idea of alternating motion (one leg, then the other) that she'll need to master in order to crawl. You'll enjoy the face-to-face time that this activity allows, too.

# 21

## sing a sweet lullaby

When your baby fusses, sing the time-honoured
lullaby "Hush, Little Baby" to relax him.

*Hush, little baby, don't say a word,*
*Papa's gonna buy you a mockingbird*

*And if that mockingbird won't sing,*
*Papa's gonna buy you a diamond ring*

*And if that diamond ring turns brass,*
*Papa's gonna buy you a looking glass*

*And if that looking glass gets broke,*
*Papa's gonna buy you a billy goat*

*And if that billy goat won't pull,*
*Papa's gonna buy you a cart and bull*

*And if that cart and bull fall down,*
*You'll still be the sweetest little baby in town.*

# 22

## dance to the beat

Dancing with babies is an age-old technique for helping them fall asleep or settle down. It provides them with the swaying motion and physical contact that they crave.

Some babies enjoy lullabies; others prefer rock'n'roll. Whatever your baby's preference, swaying with her held in your arms is a great way to bond, and it does wonders to both calm a child and ease a stressed parent's soul. In years to come, hearing the music that you and your baby danced to will bring back tender memories.

# 23

"let me play on a blanket...
When I lie on my tummy, I can
stretch out my arms and legs, lift
my head, and wave my hands."

# 24

## soar like an aeroplane

Hold your baby beneath his tummy with his
face looking downwards. For many infants, this
position is particularly soothing when they've
got wind or are very tired. Gently move him up and
down for a soothing and fun "aeroplane" ride.

# 25

## make nappy changes playful

The chore of changing nappies can also be a playful
ritual. Give your baby a clean nappy to hold, and take it
back with a cheery "thank you". Then sing "up goes the
bottom" and "on goes the nappy" as you change her.
Just as a bedtime routine can help coax her to sleep, a
well-honed nappy routine can encourage co-operation.

# 26

## smack your lips

Soft lip-smacking sounds soothe many jangled babies. The late anthropologist Ashley Montagu wrote in his book *Touching: The Human Significance of the Skin,* "The infant identifies the sounds and the lips from which they emerge with pleasurable experiences," such as being kissed.

# 27

## play with paper plates

Use your baby's attraction to faces to help him learn how to track objects visually – that is, to move his eyes and head together to follow objects. Draw a simple smiling face on a paper plate or a round piece of paper. Holding the drawing 20 to 38 cm (8 to 15 in) in front of his face, slowly move it from side to side.

# 28

## make contact

Young babies thrive on the warmth of another human. One Swedish study showed that newborn babies who were given skin-to-skin contact with their mothers cried far less than those who were not. A recent South African report also found that babies given skin-to-skin contact stayed warmer and breathed more easily than those who spent their first days in incubators. Even beyond the newborn stage, contact between baby and parent provides deep emotional and physical comfort.

# 29

## follow the fish

Set your baby in front of a fish tank
in a pet shop, at an aquarium, or at
home. Watching the fish dart this way
and that will amuse her and help her
learn to track objects with her eyes.

# 30

## blow gently

Lightly blowing on your baby's skin heightens his sense of touch. Blow on his fingers, tummy, and toes while changing his nappy. It might provide a helpful distraction if he gets impatient during the process – and it might even inspire a smile.

# 31

## listen to wind chimes

Hearing is the first sense that develops fully in a newborn baby (even foetuses can hear while in the womb). Wind chimes stimulate hearing (not to mention the sense of seeing), and your baby will love listening to the tinkling sounds, while watching the dangling pieces sway in the breeze.

# 32

## satisfy by smiling

Smile often at your baby. This simple act makes her feel special and shows her she's loved. When she learns to smile back, you'll feel loved, too.

# 33

## blow on a pinwheel

The whirring movement and flashing colours of a pinwheel mesmerize even very young babies – and at about three months of age, they might try to grab the spinning wheel. To give your baby the best view, hold the pinwheel about 60 cm (2 ft) from his face and blow on it. Don't let him hold it, though, as the edges of a pinwheel could be sharp.

# 34

## snuggle and sway

Cradle an unsettled baby upright chest-to-chest to soothe her with enclosing full-body contact. Gently rock or sway, while the baby looks out over your shoulder. Or snuggle her up under your chin where she'll feel gentle vibrations as you talk or hum.

# 35

## encourage daydreaming

With all the emphasis on actively engaging babies, keep in mind that they are sometimes content to simply daydream, just like grown-ups. If your baby is gazing at his mobile or practising lifting and lowering his tiny hand, let him enjoy the quiet time. He's not only learning to entertain himself, he's also increasing his ability to concentrate.

# 36

## read to your infant

While your newborn baby won't understand the stories you read to her, she will love being nestled in your arms and listening to the rise and fall of your voice. And studies show that because babies who are read to during infancy hear more words, they typically develop a larger vocabulary when they are older.

# 37

## say his name often

Your newborn has no concept of who he is, or even that he's a separate being with his own name. Tell him his name often – and with tenderness in your voice. It will help him learn that he's both loved and unique.

# 38

## lull with a lullaby

Singing to your baby as she drifts off to sleep is a time-tested and cherished ritual. Here's a soothing version of Brahms' lullaby to add to your bedtime repertoire.

*Lullaby and good night,*
*in the sky stars are bright.*
*Round your head, flowers gay,*
*bring you slumbers today.*
*Go to sleep now and rest,*
*may these hours be blessed.*
*Go to sleep now and rest,*
*may these hours be blessed.*

# 39

## blink your eyes

Stare directly at your baby and blink your eyes rapidly. It might just make him smile – and may give your little imitator something new to try.

# 40

## massage your newborn baby

The pressure and motion of a gentle massage help young babies' immature digestive and circulatory systems develop. At a time when you're relaxed and your baby is receptive, remove her clothes. Rub an unscented, natural, edible oil like almond, grapeseed, or olive between your hands. Gently touch and knead her arms, legs, back, and tummy. (Avoid products with mineral oil, which can leave a greasy film and block pores, and peanut oil, in case your baby is allergic.)

41

"make faces at me...
Since I was just hours old,
I've imitated your facial
expressions, from big smiles
to wide-eyed surprise."

# 42

## hold fingers

Your infant's grasp reflex makes him curl his tiny fingers around your finger when you stroke his palm. While this response is pure reflex, letting your baby hold your fingers promotes attachment and introduces him to the pleasure of touch.

# 43

## dangle the ribbons

Indulge your baby's growing interest in movement and colour. Tie several short ribbons about 15 cm (6 in) long onto a bracelet or plastic clothes hanger. Flutter the ribbons in front of her, letting them tickle her arms and legs. As she grows older, she'll reach out to touch the captivating ribbons.

# 44

## name that part

After a bath, teach your baby the names of body parts by gently running some soft terry towelling all over his body, naming each stop on the tour.

# 45

## smell the roses

Your baby was born with an extremely refined sense of smell. Immediately after birth, babies can even recognize the smell of their mothers. Indeed, one way newborn babies find their mother's nipple is through scent. Stimulate your infant's sense of smell by passing pleasantly scented objects, such as flowers, oranges, or vanilla extract, beneath her nose. She can't sniff voluntarily (that doesn't happen until about 18 months of age), but she'll enjoy smelling sweet scents in the air.

# 46

## cruise in your car

Many fractious babies calm down and even fall asleep
when they're driven around in a car. Sometimes that
effect kicks in after 5 minutes; sometimes it takes
15 minutes or more. See if your baby is soothed into
slumber by a car ride – and have an audiobook or CD
handy to keep yourself entertained along the way.

# 47

## travel with toys

On some days, a bag full of goodies may be the one
thing that will keep your baby (and you!) from having
meltdowns in the car. Fill the bag with rattles, board
books, and toys, and change the contents often so
you'll always have a new diversion readily to hand.

# 48

## put it in black and white

Your newborn baby can see the high contrast of simple large black-and-white patterns more easily than the subtle shades of brightly coloured ones. To help stimulate his vision, hang black-and-white images – a mobile or framed fabric, for example – where he can see them. By about two months of age, your baby will be able to note the subtle shades of grey almost as well as you can.

# 49

## swing together

The peaceful swaying of a hammock relaxes babies and stimulates their vestibular system, the body's mechanism for maintaining balance and sensing movement through space. If your hammock is woven out of rope, cover it with a thick towel to make your baby's head and back more comfortable and to keep her hands and feet safely out of the webbing. Don't leave your baby alone or fall asleep with her in the hammock, however, because if she rolls into you she may not be able to lift her head to breathe.

# 50

## shake the rattles

Once your baby has demonstrated an ability to grasp things, he'll enjoy holding and shaking light rattles. His first rattle-shaking will be involuntary. But hearing the rattling sound will help him eventually learn that cause (moving the toy) creates effect (noise). Start with light plastic or cloth rattles; heavy rattles are too difficult for young babies to hold, and they can hit themselves on the head with them.

# 51

## sing a scrub-a-dub song

Sing this simple ditty to the tune of "Frère Jacques"
to entertain your baby during bath time.

*Now we're washing*
*Now we're washing*
*Baby's toes*
*Baby's toes.*
*Now we're washing knees and*
*Now we're washing elbows*
*And baby's nose*
*And baby's nose.*

# 52

## bathe with baby

Taking a bath together is one of life's great pleasures — for baby and parent alike. Cradle your baby in your arms, play little splashing games, and experiment with textured cloths and sponges. The water should be warm but not hot. Before you get out of the bath, hand your baby to another grown-up or place her on a thick towel near the bath (never stand up with a wet, slippery baby in your hands).

# 53

"rub my toes...
It increases my circulation
and makes me aware of where
my body begins and ends."

# 54

## tease the "piggies"

This traditional game will delight your child.

*This little piggy went to market*
gently tug a different toe with each line

*This little piggy stayed at home*

*This little piggy had roast beef*

*This little piggy had none*

*And this little piggy cried*

*"Whee, whee, whee!" all the way home.*
tickle his tummy with "Whee, whee, whee!"

# 55

## play peekaboo

Look at your baby. Now look away. Look at him again,
then look away. Sneak another peek – and look away.
Now listen! He'll call you back with gurgles and coos.

# 56

## build some bedtime routines

In the big, surprising world, babies love the security of rituals and repetition, especially when it's time to go to sleep. As you and your baby develop a bedtime routine, include activities that your baby finds absorbing but not too exciting. Practical preparations might include a warm relaxing bath or spot-cleaning, followed by putting on fresh pyjamas. It's never too early to start a bedtime reading habit, as a couple of short books can help lull a child to sleep. Then move on to soft music, a soothing lullaby, a feeding, or a comforting cuddle in the rocking chair. Consider starting a custom of talking about the day's events — the conversation won't be one-sided for long. Once your child settles into a routine, it can provide continuity at bedtime for months, even years, to come.

57

# mesmerize with a mobile

By about two months of age, babies are intrigued by
musical mobiles. With their swirling, colourful objects
and soothing melodies, these toys stimulate both
vision and hearing. Entertain your infant by hanging
a mobile above her cot or changing table. To ensure
that your baby never gets caught up in the mobile's
strings, keep it at least an adult arm's length away.

# 58

## sing with the spider

While he won't be able to mimic your hand motions until he's about a year old, your baby will love listening to the travails of "The Insey-Winsey Spider". Add tactile stimulation by crawling the spider up his tummy, "pouring" the rain down his shoulders, and crossing his arms over his head to make the sun come out.

*The insey-winsey spider went up the water spout,*
"walk" your fingers up in the air

*Down came the rain and washed the spider out.*
wiggle your fingers downwards to make rain

*Out came the sun and dried up all the rain,*
form a circle with your hands above your head

*And the insey-winsey spider went up the spout again.*
"walk" your fingers up again

# 59

## play with shadows

Because babies are intrigued by moving objects as well as by light and dark patterns, shadows tend to fascinate them, too. In a darkened room, shine a torch on your baby's mobile or wiggle your fingers in front of a lamp to cast shadows on a wall. Watch as her eyes widen and her feet kick with glee.

# 60

## mix things up

Babies lose interest when shown the same thing too often. So occasionally hang new pictures near the cot, introduce a new rattle, or find a soft toy that has a different squeak. Slightly changing your baby's environment once in a while will help heighten his awareness of his surroundings.

# 61

## rock the night away

Never underestimate the calming properties of the
time-honoured rocking chair. Together, you and your
baby can rock away the stresses of a stimulating day.
Your baby will hear your voice, feel your warmth, and
perhaps even drowse on your shoulder. She'll also begin
to feel rhythm from the steady rocking of the chair, and
understanding rhythm is essential to learning language.

# 62

## come when he calls

Responding to your baby's cries teaches him that he
has some control over his world, that people love him,
and that it's safe to trust those who care for him. Don't
worry, you can't spoil a young baby. You can only
assure him that his wants and needs matter.

# 63

## bounce for fun

An infant will enjoy a gentle bouncing ride on your knee, as long as she can hold her own head up, while you carefully support her. (Just be sure you don't jiggle her too hard.) Add this jingle sung to the tune of "Mary Had a Little Lamb" to your knee ride for even more fun.

*Oh, baby's on my knee, knee, knee*
*knee, knee, knee*
*knee, knee, knee*
*Baby's on my knee, knee, knee*
*And jiggling up and down.*
bounce her lightly on your knee

*Oh, baby's going whee, whee, whee*
*whee, whee, whee*
*whee, whee, whee*
*Baby's going whee, whee, whee*
*And now she's dipping down.*
hold her to your chest and dip her slowly
backwards, while supporting her head

# 64

"kiss my tummy...
It tickles, it makes me
smile, and it teaches
me where my tummy is."

# 65

## pick the right moments

Babies are alert only for short periods of time. When
your infant is calm and attuned to his surroundings,
he'll be most likely to respond. Use these moments
to introduce him to new toys, books, and music.

# 66

## do baby sit-ups

The infant version of this exercise will help strengthen
your child's neck muscles. Simply lay her on her back
on a blanket and sit at her feet, facing her. Then firmly
grasp the top corners of the blanket with both hands
so it fits securely around her head and upper body like
a sling. Gently pull her towards you, then gently lower
her. Slowly repeat several times — until she indicates
she's tired by looking away or squirming.

# 67

## look sideways

At this age, your baby will tend to lie with his head to one side. Give him something to gaze at by placing colourful toys or simple drawings in the area where he looks. (If you use string to hang an item, make sure it's at least an adult arm's length away from the cot, so it does not pose a strangulation hazard.)

# 68

## dangle the toys

At around two months of age, your baby will start reaching for objects around her. Encourage her by holding a soft toy, a rattle, or plastic measuring spoons in front of her. Don't, however, hand an object to her too quickly or yank it out of her reach. To feel successful, she needs to aim for the toy and grasp it.

# 69

## be part of the family

It's almost impossible to spend all of your
waking hours interacting with your baby.
But you can socialize with him while
getting other things done by keeping
him in a fairly well-trafficked area of your
home. Safely tuck your baby in a pushchair
or carrycot and let him watch family
members as they go about their business
in the kitchen or living room. He can
also hear them as they pass by, which will
help him feel like he's part of the action.

# 70

## get out and about

Go on short daily trips together. You can take your baby just about anywhere — to the supermarket or the shopping centre. New sights are stimulating and will introduce her to a variety of social situations.

# 71

## stroke his hands

Help your baby become more aware of the
way his hands open and close. When his fists are
tightly clenched, stroke the back of each one, an
action that generally makes a baby relax his grip.

# 72

## change her perspective

Offer your infant a new view and strengthen her body
at the same time by propping her on her side with
rolled-up blankets or turning her over onto her tummy.
Be attuned to signs that she's uninterested or tired – for
example, if she fusses or cries. And remember, when
it's time for her to sleep, lay her on her back.

# 73

## create a baby journal

Maybe you feel you'll never forget her first fleeting smile or first bit of "ba-ba-ba" babbling. But today's memories will be crowded out by new events, as your baby keeps you in the present moment. So jot down a few notes each week documenting the discoveries and wonders of early babyhood. Keep the journal convenient, perhaps by the bed, or in your nappy-bag to use during that rare free moment in a waiting room.

Help your baby contribute some footprints or handprints, maybe even a series at three-month intervals. Use a non-toxic, washable, medium-dark stamp pad, found in your local craft shop. For a clear print, bring first the pad and then the paper firmly to the wiggly foot. Someday, when your child sees these artworks, he won't believe he was ever that small (and you won't either).

# 74

## soothe with song

She's too young to ask for a pony, but you can still please her with this melodic lullaby, "All the Pretty Little Horses".

*Hush-a-bye, don't you cry,*
*go to sleepy, little baby.*
*When you wake, you'll have*
*all the pretty little horses.*

*Black and bay, dapple and grey,*
*coach and six little horses.*
*Hush-a-bye, don't you cry,*
*go to sleepy, little baby.*

# 75

## admire sweet baby faces

British researchers recently found that babies, even newborn babies, are more attracted to designs that look like faces than any other designs. Babies examine faces with great care and as a result learn about the social cues inherent in various facial expressions. Show your baby the faces in this book and others. Which ones make him smile? Which ones puzzle him?

# 76

## greet her with joy

Your baby learns about human emotions – including happiness, sadness, and the exhilaration of seeing a loved one – primarily from her family. Show her how people greet each other by giving her a big smile and a cheerful hello – and do it often throughout the day. By watching you, she'll learn and soon imitate what you do.

# 77

## practise patience

Newborn babies need time to figure out how to do what they want to do – whether it's reaching out to grasp something, kicking at a toy, or imitating your facial expressions. Be patient during these fertile moments. If you rush to help or turn away before he's done what he's trying to do, he'll become discouraged.

# 78

## stick out your tongue

Babies are born knowing how to imitate many of the expressions they see on other faces. So try sticking out your tongue and see if your baby responds in kind. Or open your mouth wide and say "ahhhh" several times; she may open her mouth and say "ahhhh" right back.

 # 79

## bedeck him with bracelet bells

Help your baby understand that he has his own hands and assist him in getting used to how they move by putting a small colourful rattle-bracelet on his tiny wrist. Check that rattles, bells, and beads are securely attached to the bracelet to ensure that they never loosen and get into his mouth.

# 80

## hug for happiness

Numerous studies have shown that holding a baby
releases the calming hormone oxytocin (also called
the "cuddle hormone") in both parent and child.
Hold her often: it will help calm you and your
baby, as well as promote greater attachment.

# 81

## dress with success

It can be difficult – and distressing – to dress an infant
who's protesting: flopping his neck, flailing his arms,
maybe even wailing. Try singing or playing peekaboo
to distract him from the task at hand. If he doesn't like
being naked, cover him with a light blanket. Choose
easy-to-handle clothing, such as tops with wide
neckholes and trousers with elastic waists.

# 82

"lay me on a big beach ball...
Gently roll me back and forth
while holding me on top of the
ball, and I'll develop balance
and stronger neck muscles."

# 83

## set up a floor gym

Even if your infant is too young to swat at the dangling toys of a floor gym, you can still lay her beneath one so she can look up at it. She will want to touch the appealing colours and shapes so much that someday soon she'll lift an arm and start batting away.

# 84

## offer toys one at a time

As tempting as it is to give your child all of the toys, rattles, and playthings you've collected for him, hold yourself back. Since he can only hold one object at a time, having too much in his visual field may confuse or frustrate him. Give him one or two toys, and replace them when he appears bored. This will also help him focus – and prevent over-stimulation.

# 85

## make eye contact

Newborn babies can only focus on objects within 20 to 38 cm (8 to 15 in) of their nose – the perfect distance for seeing a nursing mum's face. But your baby isn't able to track an object that moves from one side to the other. (In fact, she doesn't even know yet that moving her head along with her eyes expands her view.) To help strengthen her eye muscles so they can work together, slowly move a brightly coloured object (such as a soft toy or handkerchief) back and forth in front of her. By the time she's about three months old, these exercises will tempt her to reach out and grasp the object, a result of her budding hand-eye co-ordination skills.

# 86

## give a mini-massage

If you don't have time to give your baby a
full-fledged massage, just spend a few minutes
lightly stroking him – from shoulder to wrist, thigh
to foot, and chest to tummy. You may even find that
your baby prefers this to deeper massage strokes.

# 87

## encourage head lifts

You are the best incentive to get your baby to
practise lifting her head, which will help strengthen
her neck muscles. When she's on her tummy,
position yourself so that she'll see your face if she
lifts her head. Call her name to entice her to look
up. This exercise may frustrate some babies, so
watch for any telltale signs of distress.

# 3+

## three months & up

Sometimes called the honeymoon period, the second three months of your baby's life are a time of glorious smiles, belly laughs, exploring hands, and joyfully kicking feet. Many babies learn to sit during this stage, a core skill that allows them to see the world more clearly and to manipulate objects with greater precision. Most infants are picking up crucial social skills now, too, such as how to babble, giggle, and smile.

# 88

## meet ms. spoon and mr. fork

If your baby is getting restless in a restaurant, introduce him to Mr. Fork and Ms. Spoon. Make the fork and spoon dance, talk, and pop out from behind the napkin dispenser, the nappy-bag, or the menu. Your baby will laugh and laugh — and you'll get good practice in improvisation!

# 89

## swing and rock

This classic poem by Robert Louis Stevenson becomes
the perfect accompaniment to rocking your baby.

*How do you like to go up in a swing*
rock your baby back and forth gently in your arms

*Up in the air so blue?*
stop while holding her high on one side

*Oh, I do think it the pleasantest thing*
rock your baby back and forth again

*Ever a child can do!*
stop while holding her high on the other side

# 90

## enchant with a music box

He won't be dexterous enough to wind a music box
on his own, but your baby will enjoy hearing its tinkling
tune and watching the magical twirling figurine.

# 91

## prop up your baby

Your baby's muscle control develops from top to bottom: first her neck strengthens; then her upper back, middle back, and lower back; and finally her hips and legs. But even before her muscles can support her body, her mind focusses on the idea of sitting. (That's why she will lift her head off her nappy-changing table and pull herself up by grabbing your hands.) To help her get a start on sitting, prop her up with several large pillows. The cushioned support helps her develop balance and muscle strength, and keeps her from getting hurt if she falls over. As an added benefit, she also gets a different vantage point on the world: she's looking at life head-on, instead of from a prone position.

# 92

## marvel at the supermarket

At about three months of age, your baby is the perfect companion for outings to the supermarket. While he still loves to be held, he's becoming increasingly interested in the world beyond the safety of your arms. Let him ogle the colourful fruits and vegetables, touch the frozen-food cabinet, and smile at others. Introduce new words during each shopping expedition, too.

# 93

## give her a play-by-play

While many noises interest your baby, it's the sound of the human voice that intrigues her most. Fill her ears with language by explaining what you're doing as you do it, whether it's washing her hair, making dinner, or organizing your files. She'll be exposed to new words – and to more of your world.

# 94

## take time to listen

After the thrill of the first coos and babbles has gone, remember that your baby still needs to practise the art of conversation. To accomplish this, make sure he has opportunities to talk to a receptive audience. Give him time to untie his tongue and get some words out – even if it's just babbling.

# 95

## put on a water show

To help your baby develop hand-eye co-ordination and fine motor skills, give her plastic drinking and measuring cups to play with in the bath. If she can't handle the pouring motion yet, do it for her, letting her enjoy the sight and sound of cascading water.

# 96

## take an exercise class

Now that your baby is more settled, you can take better care of yourself. Many health clubs offer postnatal exercise classes that welcome pre-crawling infants as well. Aerobics and yoga help new mothers get back in shape. While the parents exercise, the babies enjoy listening to the music, watching the movement, and receiving the kisses, tickles, and smiles sent their way.

# 97

## practise baby sign language

Many child-development experts believe that
babies can communicate with hand signs long
before they can express themselves in spoken
language. In fact, some experts say that babies
who learn to communicate with their hands feel
more confident and are less prone to frustration
than those who have no words to express their
needs and feelings. Introduce your baby to
non-verbal communication by teaching him a
simple sign for "eat": put your fingers to your
lips repeatedly each time you ask him if
he's hungry, and several times during the meal.
As with spoken language, he'll probably
understand the signal before he makes the sign
himself, but in a few weeks, you'll see him bring
his hand to his lips when he's hungry.

# 98

"let me touch things...
I like to feel silk, satin,
a smooth round stone,
feathers, felt, and
a rough pine cone."

# 99

## move up and down

To demonstrate the spatial meaning of up and down, say "up" when lifting your baby and say "down" when lowering her. Use a high-pitched voice on the way up and a lower-pitched tone on the way down, so she'll start to understand that voices go up and down, too.

# 100

## go bare

A baby newborn's skin may be too sensitive for this activity, but many three- to six-month-old babies love it: undress your child so he can delight in the feel of a warm breeze on his bare skin, a soft rug on his tummy, or the grass tickling his toes. As long as he's warm and not in direct sunlight, hanging out naked for a while is a great way for him to become aware of his body.

# 101

## get bubbly

Shimmering soap bubbles, floating just beyond reach, are one of the many delights of childhood. They also serve a purpose: by watching bubbles, babies strengthen their ability to visually track and focus on objects. And by trying to touch them, they boost their hand-eye co-ordination.

# 102

## whistle a tune

While talking is a long way off, your little one is tuning in to your familiar voice and starting to discern the everyday consonants and vowels that pass your lips. So surprise her by making eye contact and producing some unexpected sounds, such as briskly whistling or chirping.

# 103

## size him up

Ask your baby, "How big are you?" Then stretch his arms gently over his head and say, "Sooo big! Sooo big!" This promotes flexibility and body awareness – and promises to make him smile.

# 104

## roll her over

Your baby will learn to roll over at around five or six months. While this is a natural development, you can help her gain the strength, co-ordination, and confidence this move requires. To get her used to the motion, place her on her back on a blanket. Then gently lift one edge of the blanket so she starts to roll slowly over onto one side. After practising this a few times, try rolling her in the opposite direction.

# 105

## sing loudly and softly

Introduce your baby to the notion of loud and soft volumes with the ditty "John Jacob Jingleheimer Schmidt". Sing this verse over and over, more quietly each time, until you're just moving your lips — except for the last line, which should always be sung with great gusto.

*John Jacob Jingleheimer Schmidt,*
*His name is my name too.*
*Whenever we go out,*
*The people always shout,*
*"There goes John Jacob Jingleheimer Schmidt!"*
*Tah, dah, dah, dah, dah, dah, dah!*

# 106

## prepare to tap-dance

To help your baby get a sense of rhythm (as well as a better idea of what his magical feet can do), tap his toes along to the beat of a song. Soon he'll start tapping and kicking his feet on his own whenever he hears music he likes.

# 107

## create a hand puppet

You have the makings of a puppet right at hand —
actually, it is your hand. Curl your index finger into your
thumb to form an O. Draw on eyes, then adopt a funny
voice and move your fingers to make the face "talk". Your
fascinated baby may even try to make her hand talk back!

# 108

## introduce the big kids

If you don't have other children in your household,
visit friends with older kids or spend time at the
playground observing the three- and four-year-olds.
Your baby will love to see what bigger, stronger kids
can do. Keep him on the sidelines, rather than in
the centre of the action, so he's not at risk of being
accidentally knocked over in all the hubbub.

# 109

## talk to the animals

Your baby is becoming aware of both the concept of
language and the differences between animals. It's
now the ideal time to introduce her to the language
of animals: as you read books together, play with soft
toys, or greet pets, make each animal's signature
noise, be it *miaow, woof, moo, squeak,* or *roar!*

110

## make mealtime fun

Babies eat while being held in loving arms, and soon
learn that meals aren't just about food. Feedings offer
quiet times for eye contact and chats. Even before your
baby starts eating solid foods, bring him to the family
table, seated on a lap or in a highchair, and provide
unbreakable bowls, cups, and utensils to wave and
mouth, so he sees that dining is also a social event.

# 111

## play with ice cubes

3+

3 months & up

The cold temperature and slippery texture of ice cubes fascinate babies at this age. Make sure the ice is too large to pose a choking hazard. To make oversized ice blocks, freeze water in a large paper cup or milk carton, then simply peel off the wrapper.

# 112

## sneak up on her

Why young children love a friendly game of chase is one of life's great mysteries. Many relatively immobile babies also enjoy having you creep up on them – especially if you playfully announce, "I'm gonna get you!"

# 113

## team up on chores

Babies learn by tagging along and observing daily tasks. Don't wait until your baby is asleep to finish folding the washing. Let him sit on the floor amid the colourful clothes as you fold them, pausing to flap, shake, and discuss some items with your appreciative "laundry show" audience.

# 114

## touch textures

Now that your baby is fascinated with tactile things, keep her tiny fingers busy with a book of textures. Look for animal-themed board books that feature fake fur. Or create a fun-to-feel book by gluing large swatches of coarse, silky, and furry fabric onto felt pages.

# 115

## give him a lift

Your baby's perspective on the world tends to be limited to the view from the floor, cot, and pushchair. But there are many interesting things higher up, too. Carry him around and show him some sights: pictures on the wall, flowers blooming on a high-twining vine, and knick-knacks on your shelves. Let him stroke the fabric of jackets hanging in the cupboard and feel the cool glass of a window pane. Give him a chance to reach for snowflakes or the leaves on a tree branch. He'll get a big kick out of seeing – and experiencing – these discoveries.

# 116

**"bolster me...**
Put a rolled-up towel
under my small arms
to help strengthen
my back and neck.**"**

# 117

## blow raspberries

Your baby will get a kick out of this silly poem. End it by blowing a loud "raspberry" on her tummy.

*Oh, it's a terrible sound*
*When a raspberry blows.*
*It's rude and it's crude*
*And your bad manners show!*
*But it sure makes me laugh*
*And it sure makes me giggle.*
*It makes my whole body*
*Just jiggle and wiggle!*

# 118

## click your tongue

Make loud clicking sounds with your tongue against the roof of your mouth. This may make your baby smile and even inspire him to try making the sounds.

# 119

## sneeze loudly

Your infant is amazed by her body and, in particular, by the sounds she and others can make. You'll prompt a big laugh if you respond to her delicate baby sneezes with a loud, grown-up "aaaCHOOO!"

# 120

## carry him like a flagpole

To help your baby strengthen his back and abdominal muscles, hold him facing away from you while you're standing. Put one hand just above his knees and the other hand securely under his chest. Now let him lean slightly away from your body — in a position that's similar to how a marcher carries a flagpole in a parade. Some babies enjoy being held in this angled position — so see if your child gets a chuckle from it, too.

# 121

## introduce a new language

3+

3 months & up

A child is never too young to hear a new language.
One great way to start is by greeting your baby
in the morning in both French and English with
this classic song, "Frère Jacques".

*Frère Jacques, Frère Jacques,*
*Dormez-vous, dormez vous?*
*Sonnez les matines,*
*Sonnez les matines.*
*Ding, ding, dong.*
*Ding, ding, dong.*

*Are you sleeping, are you sleeping,*
*Brother John, Brother John?*
*Morning bells are ringing,*
*Morning bells are ringing.*
*Ding, ding, dong.*
*Ding, ding, dong.*

# 122

## whisper sweet rhymes

During your baby's bedtime routine, dim the lights,
carry her to a window with a view of the sky,
and murmur this traditional sleeptime rhyme.

*Come to the window,*
*My baby with me,*
*And look at the stars*
*That shine on the sea!*
*There are two little stars*
*That play hide-and-seek*
*With two little fish*
*Far down in the deep.*
*And two little frogs*
*Cry "Neap, neap, neap."*
*I see a dear baby*
*Who should be asleep.*

# 123

## sing to the tune of a classic

Introduce your child to some simple fingerplays
while singing this starry song to the tune
of "Row, Row, Row Your Boat".

*One, two, three big stars*
count to three with your
fingers on one hand

*Blinking in the sky!*
open and close both of your hands
three times to make them "blink"

*Twinkle, twinkle, twinkle, twinkle*
continue "blinking" both hands while
raising them over your head

*How'd they get so high?*
hold out your hands, palms up, as
if you don't know the answer

# 124

## bring a sock to life

For instant baby amusement, put your
hand inside a sock and open and close
its "mouth" while speaking in a funny
voice. This impromptu puppet show
makes a great diversion when you're
changing your baby's clothes or even
while queuing at the supermarket checkout.

# 125

## double the noise

Soft squeaky toys instantly reward your baby's new grasping skills. Give him a toy for each hand. Can he hold onto both yet? Does he look at the toy that's making the louder noise?

# 126

## explore junior-edition yoga

In baby-yoga classes, your little one lies on her back or tummy, or in your arms, while you guide her body into adapted poses, sometimes with rhymes, songs, swaying, or gentle bouncing. Several books outline the basics, although you and your baby may enjoy the sociability of a class.

# 127

## share family songs

Friends and family are often eager to help new parents but may not know how. So they might be delighted if you ask them to share some favourite songs and rhymes that they used to sing to their wee ones – maybe even versions in another language. If Grandma shares a few songs that her grandmother sang to her as a child or that an uncle hummed to you or your spouse, you're likely to develop a special connection to the song when you share it with your baby. And you can tell him its history when he's older (and maybe when he's grown-up he'll even sing it to his own offspring).

# 128

## put bells on baby's toes

Buy or make socks or ankle bracelets adorned with bells and rattles. These encourage your baby to kick to hear the pleasing noise. (Make sure anything sewn onto your baby's clothing is securely fastened so it can't come off and pose a choking hazard.)

**3+**

3 months & up

# 129

## make a ruckus

By three months of age, your baby is able to locate the source of nearby sounds. To help her develop this skill, move around the room while talking in funny voices or making a toy squeak or rattle. Praise her efforts as she looks, squirms, and even wriggles over to the spot where you're making all those interesting noises.

# 130

## cheer on the bouncing baby

When your baby uses your hands to pull himself upright and starts bouncing, encourage him. Many babies can do this for long stretches of time, and that's fine – it's a great way for them to strengthen their leg muscles and boost self-esteem. (There's also the benefit of giving your arms a good workout!)

# 131

## roll for the toy

Tempt your baby to reach out and grasp things by placing a toy just off to the side of where she's lying. As she gets older, place the toy a bit further away, which will inspire her to roll over to reach it.

# 132

**"laugh at my giggles...**
Show me that I'm a special baby
and that my joy delights you — and
how laughter, like all good things,
is best when shared.**"**

# 133

## start swinging

Once your baby can sit up with a bit of support, he's ready to try a ride in a bucket-seat swing. Depending on his sitting skills, you can place him towards the rear of the seat or slump him forward over the front with a rolled blanket behind him for more support. Push him gently and not too high at first – his neck may not be able to handle racing forwards and backwards. If he enjoys the sensation of swinging, spice up his ride by tickling his leg or kissing his cheek each time he comes forward. Swinging helps develop the vestibular system, the body's mechanism for maintaining balance and monitoring its movements. These skills are crucial for learning to crawl, walk, run, ride a bike – just about any activity that entails movement.

# 134

## crush some crisps

Stuck in a queue at the supermarket? Hand your baby
a sealed bag of potato crisps to crinkle and crush (but
not to eat). She'll be diverted for at least a little while
by the sound and texture of her new "toy" – a small
price to pay to avoid a potential meltdown.

**3+**

3 months & up

# 135

## ask questions

Engage your baby by asking him questions. These can
be the pleasantries of small talk: "How are you?" or
"Isn't it a lovely day?" Or they can be more specific:
"Are you warm in that coat?" Wait for your baby to
answer even if his response is just a string of babbled
sounds. This teaches him the rhythm of conversation.
In a few years, he'll be the one asking the questions!

# 136

## vary the carrying

Car seats that can be moved from car to pushchair to
house, while convenient, don't offer a baby much
physical stimulation. All infants need and love to
be held. And a baby sling is a great way for them
to travel, as a parent's arms are the safest and most
interesting place to be. After all, caring touch is
a powerful form of communication.

# 137

## seek special recognition

Naturally you long to hear your baby say your name.
So when he babbles "ma-ma" or "da-da," respond with
a smile and say "Here's Mummy!" or "Here's Daddy!"
He'll see that some sounds get big responses.

# 138

## appreciate books in a new way

You want your baby to look at the pictures and enjoy listening to the story in her new board book, but she has other ideas: she pops the book right into her mouth. Don't worry — children's board and cloth books are made to withstand some baby gumming action. And at this stage, your child will explore much of her environment by putting things in her mouth. So let her gum books to her heart's delight. Eventually she'll explore them with her hands, eyes, and mind, too!

# 139

## give him a concert

Your baby's fascination with sound (and with you) means that he'll be a rapt audience as you play an instrument. Experiencing how music is created – not just hearing it on a tape, a CD, or the radio – will help cultivate his interest in music. Allow him to touch the instrument. Plucking guitar strings, banging a drum, or pressing the keys of a bugle teaches him about cause and effect and lets him feel involved. And when families play music together, children learn that music is an art form anyone can enjoy.

# 140

## sing to amuse her

Sing this endearing peekaboo song, "Where Is Baby?", to the tune of "Frère Jacques".

*Where is baby?*
*Where is baby?*
cup hands around your eyes as if searching

*Where can she be?*
*Where can she be?*
pretend to scan the horizon, searching

*Where's my silly baby?*
*Where's my silly baby?*
shrug your shoulders and put
your hands out, palms up

*Ding dong dee!*
*Ding dong dee!*
"find" your baby and give her a kiss

# 141

## revel in quiet time

Babies are loads of fun at this stage: curious, sociable, and unbelievably cute. They love to interact, but need breaks from social stimulation, too. Don't interrupt your baby if you see her fiddling with carpet fibres, staring out of the window, or playing with her toes. Sometimes she just needs time to explore the world in a quiet way.

# 142

## give him target practice

Help your baby strengthen his leg muscles, develop foot-eye co-ordination, and just have fun by letting him kick at objects you hold near his feet. Use soft balls, soft toys, or whatever catches his eye and tempts his feet. For an added bonus, choose objects that make noise when struck, so your baby learns about cause and effect.

# 143

## react to her cough

At about five months of age, lots of babies make an exciting discovery: they learn how to cough on purpose to get the attention of grown-ups. Once you're sure your little actor is coughing for effect and not because she's ill or choking, play along with her antics. Try imitating her after she gives a little cough, or putting your hands on your cheeks in wide-eyed surprise. She'll repeat her action often to prompt your humorous responses.

# 144

**"play a tickle game...**
It's so great when you tickle and giggle with me. My favourite part is guessing where you'll tickle next: fingers, toes, belly, or nose?**"**

# 145

## pop a bubble

Elicit glee and giggles by blowing a big
chewing-gum bubble for your baby.
Then – *snap!* – pop it back into your mouth.

# 146

## mimic each other

Your baby has shown you that he can stick out his
tongue and smile to copy your expressions. He may
even be imitating some of your sounds (like "ma-ma"
and "ba-ba"). Introduce a new mimicking game by
showing him how to open his mouth wide or how to
blow raspberries, then watch to see if he'll join in.

# 147

## let her get mouthy

Allow your baby to suck on your sleeve, gum her soft blocks, and stick her big, noisy rattle in her mouth. Once you get beyond the drool factor and the fear of germs, you'll see that her mouth is one of her primary tools of exploration. So let her use it to learn about the world — just make sure that nothing sharp, toxic, or small enough to swallow is within reach.

# 148

## turn up the volume

As your baby begins to babble, he'll also start experimenting with the volume of his voice. Without startling him, show him how your own voice can get louder — as well as quieter. He may try to copy you.

# 149

## talk about body parts

By frequently repeating the names of body parts to your baby, you'll help her learn what her body does and build her receptive vocabulary (the number of words she understands). Try to use body-part names in the course of everyday speech, rather than in a dull recitation. For example, instead of saying "These are your toes, and these are your hands", try something like "Let's get these little toes into your socks", or "Are your hands sticky?" – and emphasize the word you are teaching her. This builds her vocabulary and introduces more complex sentence structures.

# 150

## kiss the toes

Your baby will giggle with delight if you
recite this ditty while kissing his toes.
*One, two, three, four, five*
*Hey, baby! These toes are alive!*

# 151

## play with parachutes

Babies and young children love experimenting with
fabrics – whether it's a scarf billowing high above
a child's head or a huge lightweight cloth that kids
pull over themselves to create a canopy. To make a
parachute suitable for your baby, drape a sheet, scarf,
or thin blanket over your tiny adventurer's head, then
whisk it off again – sometimes quickly, sometimes
slowly. She'll enjoy this tactile version of peekaboo.

# 152

## make a mobile that's mobile

Even though your baby's ability to focus on things in the distance is improving, he'll often prefer to look at details nearby. To provide a choice, securely attach colourful, lightweight objects to the pushchair cover so they dangle just out of his reach. Keep them on top of the cover while he enjoys the scenery, and flip them down into view when he gets restless.

3+

3 months & up

# 153

## create light shows

Help your baby strengthen her focus and visual tracking abilities by shining a torch on the wall in a darkened room. Try moving the light up to the ceiling, then down the wall, creeping closer to her. She may even try to reach out and touch the light!

# 154

## rhyme in the rain

Singing in the rain to your bundle of joy is great fun with favourites like "Little Ducky Duddle".

*Little Ducky Duddle*
*went wading in a puddle,*
*wading in a puddle so small.*
*Said he, "It doesn't matter*
*how much I splash and splatter,*
*I'm only a ducky, after all."*

# 155

## boogie to the music

Dance with your baby to lively music. Have someone stop the music and yell, "Freeze!" Stop dancing – and watch his face light up at the sudden change. When the music starts again, resume dancing. Repeat this stop-and-start routine – he'll giggle each time you stop.

# 156

## encourage crawling

Your infant may be wriggling across the floor or rocking back and forth on her hands and knees with a clear desire to get moving. Help her get the front of her body and the back end working together by placing desirable objects, such as favourite toys, just out of her reach. This encourages her to be aware of objects as well as of her own body, and tests out her pre-crawling skills. Soon her urge to grab the objects will overcome her confusion about the mechanics of how to get there – and she'll succeed!

# 157

## bounce for balance

It may seem impossible for a baby to develop a sense of balance when he has just two main positions: lying down and sitting. The key is making sure he has plenty of opportunities to move around, too. Spinning, rocking, and bouncing all develop the vestibular system in the inner ear, which is responsible for a sense of balance and an awareness of where the body is in space. To gently stimulate that part of your baby's ears, put him on a bed (lying down, sitting, or "standing" with support) and very gently bounce the mattress.

# 158

## play footsie

Combine gentle tickles with this playful rhyme.

*Shoe a little horse*
pat the bottom of your baby's right foot

*Shoe a little mare*
pat the bottom of your baby's left foot

*But let the little coltie go bare, bare, bare!*
tickle the bottoms of both feet

# 159

## tickle her fancy

Try another little rhyme with a ticklish finish.

*Round and round the garden, with my teddy bear*
circle your baby's belly with your index finger

*One step, two step — tickle her under there!*
"walk" your fingers up and tickle under her chin

# 160

## prepare him to crawl

Put your baby on his tummy for this pre-crawling exercise. Gently push one foot towards his body, then the other. He'll learn to push his foot against your hand, which will thrust him forwards – ever so slightly at first. As he gets used to the exercise, he'll cover more ground with each push and get a clearer idea of how this crawling business actually works.

# 161

## explore a garden

While babies can't tell the difference between tulips and ferns, they recognize a beautiful place when they see it. Spend time with your baby in gardens or parks; she'll be enchanted by the waving branches, colourful blooms, singing birds, and wonderful smells.

# 162

" what a big world this is...
Tell me about everything I
see – from your funny red hat
to that large black cat. "

# 163

## toss a beach ball

Enchant your baby with the motion and colour of
a gently tossed inflatable beach ball. Lay him on
his back, then throw the ball in the air and catch it
above him – again and again. He'll love watching
it sail through the air – and he'll enjoy the surprise
of seeing you catch it just before it reaches him.

# 164

## saddle up for a knee ride

Sit your baby facing towards you on your knees, and hold her securely around her middle as you treat her to a lively — but gentle — knee ride. As she rides, vary your tempo, pitch, and volume.

*The farmer's horse goes ho-dee-ho, ho-dee-ho*
gently sway your baby forwards and backwards,
as if she's on a very fat, waddling horse

*The lady's horse goes trip-trop, trip-trop*
alternate bouncing each knee
slowly up and down

*The gentleman's horse goes trot-trot, trot-trot*
simultaneously bounce both knees
quickly up and down

*But* (say your baby's name) *horse goes
gallopy, gallopy, gallopy, gallopy!*
alternate bouncing each knee
quickly up and down

# 165

## pop like popcorn

Your baby will smile at this sprightly fingerplay,
even though he's too young to eat popcorn.

*I woke up this morning*
stretch your arms above your
head, as if awakening

*And what did I see?*
frame your eyes with your hands
as if looking through binoculars

*Popcorn popping on my apple tree!*
quickly raise and lower your arms several
times while opening and shutting
your hands (like popping corn)

*Spring has brought me a big surprise*
continue to raise and lower your arms while
opening and shutting your hands

*Popcorn popping right before my eyes!*
continue opening and shutting your hands

# 166

## trot like a pony

Hold your baby securely on one knee. Gently raise it up and down as you chant this nursery rhyme.

*Ride a cockhorse to Banbury Cross*
*To see a fine lady upon her white horse.*
*With rings on her fingers and bells on her toes,*
*She shall hear music wherever she goes.*

# 167

## rock out

Infants enjoy listening to much more than so-called baby music. Experiment with a variety of lively songs from your own music collection to find out what your child likes most. Encourage your little dancer to kick and wave her arms whenever you turn on the tunes.

# 168

## entertain with sounds

Your babbling baby enjoys repeating sounds. But he might be surprised to hear you do the same. Try repeating, with gusto, a single, fairly silly word (like "banana"), for a startled reaction or maybe a belly laugh from your little linguist.

# 169

## teach her to sit

It takes some time for babies to learn how to balance on their bottoms well enough to sit. You can help your infant gain stability by putting her legs in a diamond-shaped position. Move her heels closer to her bottom, bending her knees out to the sides. With a wider base, she's less likely to topple.

# 170

## fashion a toy-blanket

At the local toy shop, you've probably seen play-blankets with sewn-on flaps, unbreakable mirrors, and assorted fabrics. These toy-blankets enliven tummy-time and encourage reaching and exploring. You can make your own by sewing together large squares of colourful, assorted, very tactile fabrics – velvet, corduroy, fleece, vinyl, satin, or canvas. (Make sure the pieces are all washable, and pre-wash them before assembling.) Sew the patchwork onto a heavyweight piece of cloth as a backing. Stitch on a few loops to firmly secure rattles, the back covers of cloth books, and teething rings. Then let your baby explore this easily portable play area.

# 171

## swing around the clock

Your baby will enjoy swinging from
side to side like the pendulum of a
cuckoo clock, even if he won't be
able to tell the time for years to come.

*Tick tock, tick tock*
hold your baby securely under his arms
and gently swing him from side to side

*I'm a little cuckoo clock.*
continue swinging

*Tick tock, tick tock*
continue swinging

*Now I'm striking one o'clock.*
lift your baby above your head one time

*Cuckoo! Cuckoo!*
swing him from side to side

repeat by adding two o'clock and
three o'clock, and lifting up your baby
two and three times, respectively

# 172

## have fun with fingerplays

Add hand gestures to the song "Yankee Doodle"
to make it even more fun for your little one.

*Yankee Doodle went to town,*
"walk" the fingers of one of your hands
across the palm of the other

*A-riding on a pony,*
pretend to hold onto the reins of a bridle

*Stuck a feather in his cap*
mime sticking a feather in a hat

*And called it "macaroni".*
whirl your index finger around in a circle

# 6+

## six months & up

By now your baby is a charmingly social creature, one who laughs and calls out to provoke a response or win your attention. He's also a mobile baby who can roll over, and is beginning to creep, crawl, and pull himself up to get what he wants. He will test his emerging fine motor skills by fiddling with his toys or food. And he's starting to understand that objects exist even when they aren't visible: a conceptual milestone that lets him be an active participant — rather than a spectator — in hiding games like peekaboo.

# 173

## take a rainy-day walk

Grandma may scold; a neighbour may shake his head. But letting your baby feel a little rain on a mild day is perfectly safe, perfectly legal, and perfectly delightful. It stimulates her sense of touch, smell, and taste, and can promote bonding as you and your baby explore the wet world beyond your front door. Make sure her rain gear keeps her warm and dry – only her face and hands should be peeping out!

6+

6 months & up

# 174

## create a rainbow

Show your baby how a prism can turn sunlight into
a shimmering rainbow. Hang the prism in front of a
bright window, or hold it in your hand and make the
light dance around the room. Or try adjusting a glass of
water on a sunny windowsill until it creates a rainbow
(which he might try to grab) on the floor.

# 175

## make a family photo album

Strengthen the bond your baby feels with the rest of
her family by filling an album with photos of people
she knows and loves. Add pictures of beloved pets
and toys, too, and you'll have a book that will
engage and entertain her for years to come.

# 176

## go barefoot

Once your baby starts standing up with your assistance, you may be tempted to keep shoes on his feet whenever he's not napping. Going barefoot, however, is the best way for an infant to learn how his little feet work. It also makes it easier for him to work out how to rock back and forth to find the "sweet spot" that gives him balance, because he'll be able to feel the subtle contractions of the muscles that keep him upright.

Slip non-skid socks on your baby's feet if they are cold, and put shoes on if he's treading on a surface where sharp objects might be present. But if he's indoors or outdoors on a safe surface, he'll be fine going barefoot.

6+

6 months & up

# 177

## march with the duke

"The Grand Old Duke of York" will elicit giggles as your baby accompanies the Duke on his adventure.

*Oh, the Grand Old Duke of York. He had 10,000 men.*
sit on the floor with your legs extended in front of you and gently bounce your baby on your knees

*He marched them up to the top of the hill,*
slowly bend your knees upwards, with your baby seated on them

*And he marched them down again.*
slowly lower and straighten your knees

*And when you are up, you are up,*
raise both knees

*And when you are down, you are down,*
straighten both legs

*And when you are only half-way up,*
raise both legs half-way up and pause

*You are neither up nor down!*
move legs up and down quickly

# 178

## introduce activity books

Now that your baby's fine motor skills are more developed, he'll love opening the flaps, pushing the buttons, and stroking the fake fur featured in children's activity books. Actively engaging with books — not just passively listening to the words — helps an infant develop a love of reading that can last a lifetime.

# 179

## play tug-of-war

Give your infant one end of a cloth nappy or blanket to hold, then pull gently on the other end. As she pulls, increase your resistance a tiny bit. This gentle tugging game helps her develop upper-body strength and a sense of success. (Just don't pull so hard that she'll tumble backwards if she lets go!)

# 180

## track the toy

While your baby can now track objects passing back and forth before his eyes, it's not until about his seventh month that he'll be able to follow items moving up and down. (If you drop something in front of a younger baby, he won't look down for it.) Move a toy slowly up and down about 25 cm (10 in) in front of him. See if he can follow it; if he can't, try again in a few weeks.

# 181

## experiment with sound

If your little percussionist enjoys banging on pots, treat her to a new sound by swirling a cup or two of water in a metal mixing bowl while one of you strikes it with a metal spoon. The moving water extends the bang into a wavering tone worthy of science fiction.

# 182

## fly a kite

Few toys are as magical to a child as a colourful kite soaring in the sky. While carefully supervising, allow your baby to touch the tugging string and see how it leads up to the dancing kite.

# 183

## jump to it

This game gives your baby a perfect blend of reassuring repetitions with a dash of surprise. Hold him braced against your chest, slowly chant "1...2...3...jump!", and finish with a sudden hop. Repeat, but vary the tempo, speeding up the counting, or slowing it down to create suspense leading up to the final hop.

# 184

## ring the doorbell

As your baby turns into a reckless explorer, keep quick, easy amusements on tap, such as the doorbell-distraction game. Simply scoop her up, go to the front door, and demonstrate the magic of the doorbell. Show your baby how she can press the button herself – she'll be wowed at how she can fill the place with sound.

# 185

## blow water bubbles

Using a straw, blow bubbles in a glass of water. The turbulent motion will catch your baby's attention, and the gurgling sounds will intrigue him. Don't let him try this trick himself, though, as he could poke himself with the straw or inhale the water.

# 186

## give her a security blanket

Many infants adopt what developmental psychologists call a "transitional object". It's usually a blanket or soft toy, and it gives the child something that – unlike people – doesn't come and go. So let your baby cling to, suck on, sleep with, and drag around her special object as much as she likes, since it provides a sense of continuity and reassurance.

# 187

## explore the looking glass

Hold your baby in your arms as you stand in front
of a mirror and ask, "Who's that?" Although he
won't yet understand whose reflections he's seeing,
he'll love looking at the smiling, happy faces.

# 188

## listen up!

In this auditory version of hide-and-seek, stand
behind your baby while she's playing on the floor.
Call out "Where's Mummy?" or "Where's Daddy?",
then wait for her to turn around and locate you.
When she goes back to playing, call out again
from a different location behind her.

# 189

**"**encourage me to sing...
I may just gurgle,
I may just shout,
but it's really music
I'm learning all about.**"**

# 190

## take baby steps

Hold your baby securely under his arms with
his face looking away from you, then set his feet on
top of yours and walk slowly with small steps. He'll
be thrilled to experience the joy of walking.

# 191

## perform scarf tricks

You don't have to be a magician to pull off this
trick – and you'll be helping your baby work on her
fine motor skills and hand-eye co-ordination. Simply
stuff a lightweight scarf into a kitchen-paper tube.
Then – *voilà!* – show your baby how to pull it out.
Now put it back in and let her tug it out herself.

# 192

## blow a kiss

It may take a year or two before your beloved baby can master the art of blowing a kiss. But when you blow a kiss to him, he'll understand that you're sending affection his way – and he may even enjoy trying to emulate your actions.

# 193

## listen to rain sticks

When turned upside down, these South American musical instruments – long tubes filled with beads, dried beans, or pebbles – sound like a rain shower; when shaken, they make an intriguing rattle. Rain sticks provide both auditory stimulation and the opportunity for your little rainmaker to practise her fine motor skills.

# 194

## squeeze the sponges

Give your bathing beauty a variety of body scrubbers
such as loofahs, bath mitts, and natural sponges to
play with in the bath or a big basin of water.
Squeezing water out of the sponges will stimulate his
sense of touch and strengthen his small hands.
(Always remember to closely supervise water play.)

# 195

## introduce tactile treats

Whip up a batch of coloured jelly and place
either cubes or spoonfuls on your child's highchair
tray. Then watch as your aspiring artist creates
abstract sculpture by smearing, rolling, squishing,
squashing, and smashing the shimmering stuff.

# 196

## meet mr. knickerbocker

It will be a few more months before your baby can make all the sounds in this chant, but she'll love the rhythm and enjoy watching you go through the movements.

*Hey, Mr. Knickerbocker, boppity bop!*
pat your hands on the floor once, clap, repeat

*I like the way you boppity bop!*
continue patting and clapping to establish a beat

*Listen to the sound we make with our hands.*
rub your palms together

*Listen to the sound we make with our feet.*
stomp your feet on the floor to the beat

*Listen to the sound we make with our knees.*
tap your fingers on your knees to the beat

*Listen to the sound we make with our teeth.*
click your teeth together

# 197

## devise a distraction

Rather than fight your baby's urge to grab things at the supermarket, give him a bag of marshmallows, a box of rice, or a carton of tofu to examine, squeeze, and shake while he sits in the shopping trolley. The novelty of these impromptu "toys" will keep him happily occupied (while still under your watchful eye).

# 198

## listen for clues

Hide an object that makes noise – a ticking clock, a music box, or a talking soft toy – where your adventurous crawler can find it. As she searches for the source of the sound, she'll be testing her auditory tracking skills. She'll also gain a sense of mastery when she discovers the little noisemaker.

# 199

## follow the falling leaves

Watching the twirling motion of falling leaves and hearing them crunch as the two of you step or roll on them will fascinate your baby. Let him try to catch the leaves as they fall – even if he never actually captures them, he will hone his hand-eye co-ordination.

# 200

## babble with your baby

Have you noticed how your baby tends to say her "words" in a series, such as "ba-ba-ba" and "ma-ma-ma"? Expand her listening skills and sound repertoire by introducing her to new sounds, like "ta-ta-ta" and "la-la-la". Then wait for her to respond. You're starting to teach her the art of conversation!

# 201

## knock 'em down

Your baby is not old enough to construct brick towers yet (that typically happens around 16 months of age), but he will enjoy using his hands to knock over structures that you build for him. The sight – and sound – of crashing bricks will entice your little demolition expert to do it repeatedly, so be prepared for a busy construction schedule!

# 202

## crawl together

Many babies think it's hilarious to follow a crawling parent around the house or garden – so indulge your newly mobile explorer. (And by getting a baby's-eye view of the world, you may see safety hazards you hadn't noticed before.)

# 203

## play dropsie

As your infant gains more control of her hands
and a better understanding of what they do,
she'll discover the age-old game of dropsie.
The rules are simple: baby drops object on the
floor; parent picks it up. Baby drops object
again; parent picks it up again. Tedious, right?
But look at it from your baby's point of view:
she's showing you that she understands she
has power over objects and can influence
people's behaviour — and that's a huge
cognitive leap forwards for babykind.

# 204

"raise me up...
I love it when you help me pull
myself up so I can stand – again
and again and again!"

# 205

## build a blanket fort

Remember the makeshift forts you loved so much when you were a child of six or seven? Babies also appreciate a cosy hideaway – especially if a parent or sibling hangs out with them. Simply drape a couple of large blankets or sheets over a table or two tall chairbacks, and crawl underneath with your little camper.

# 206

## dine in the buff

Even the most adorable baby clothes lose their appeal when they're covered in oatmeal or puréed peas. So let your baby eat in the buff once in a while. Not only will it keep his clothes stain-free, but it's also fun for him. And when he smears carrots across his chest, remember that he's becoming more aware of his body.

# 207

## go jogging

Whether you're running or walking, you'll get great exercise pushing your baby in a jogging pushchair, and she'll love feeling the wind in her hair. Wait until she's about six months old, when her neck muscles are strong enough to withstand jostling. Use a pushchair made for jogging; it will have better shock absorption.

# 208

## shake it up

To graduate beyond infant rattles, make "big-kid" noisemakers by filling plastic storage containers with assorted objects: jar lids, spoons, wooden blocks (nothing small enough to be a choking hazard). Snap on the lids and listen as he shakes, rattles, and rolls.

# 209

## sing about ducks

With its counting, quacking, and mother-child story line, "Five Little Ducks" is always an engaging tune.

*Five little ducks went swimming one day*
hold up your hand and wiggle five fingers

*Over the hill and far away.*
*Mother duck said,*
*"Quack, quack, quack."*
hold your hands palm to palm, then open
and shut them three times while saying "quack"

*But only four little ducks came back.*
hold up your hand and wiggle four fingers; repeat
stanzas, decreasing the number each time until
you get to "none of the little ducks came back"

*Sad mother duck went swimming one day*
wiggle one finger

*Over the hill and far away.*
*Sad mother duck said,*
*"Quack, quack, quack."*
hold your hands palm to palm, then open
and shut them three times while saying "quack"

*And all five little ducks swam back!*

# 210

## explore a fabric tunnel

A collapsible cloth tunnel (available from some toy shops) will tempt novice and experienced crawlers alike. Crawling through it will teach your baby about spatial relations, and if you place a toy inside, she'll discover that there's even a prize at the end of the tunnel!

# 211

## add funny words

By about six months of age, babies have developed quite a sense of humour. Many can even appreciate simple word games: try adding a gorilla to the lyrics of "Old McDonald", or singing "kitty" instead of "baby" in the song "Rock-a-Bye Baby" – and watch the smiles begin.

# 212

## hide in plain sight

If your baby easily finds toys hidden under boxes or blankets, challenge his sense of perception by concealing a toy behind a transparent barrier, such as a clear cutting board. Does he try to get the toy by reaching through the cutting board – or by reaching around it?

# 213

## horse around with hats

Your baby's fascination with her own image, plus her dawning awareness that she's a unique individual, will make her a rapt audience if you set her in front of a mirror and have her model some hats. Fancy ones are fun, but even a baseball cap or a straw gardening hat will do nicely.

# 214

## turn to the flip side

Tape a bright, simple picture to a big, plain box and show it to your baby. Once you've engaged his attention, encourage him to find the picture by turning the box around. He might scoot or crawl around the box, chasing the picture that he watched you make disappear.

# 215

## tease and tickle

This game introduces your baby to the
names of body parts – and works well
as a nappy-changing distraction.

*Bug-a-boo's got feet, feet, feet*
lightly tickle your baby's feet

*Bug-a-boo's got shins*
flutter your fingers up his legs

*Bug-a-boo's got a mouth to eat*
pat your fingers on his mouth

*And Bug-a-boo's got chins!*
give him a quick tickle under his chin

# 216
## give the teddy kisses

Your baby will model your behaviour, even when
the action is directed at, say, a teddy bear: "Here's
a kiss for Teddy!" and "Here's a kiss for Baby!"

# 217
## teach him to feed himself

Do you spend more time trying to stop your baby
from grabbing his spoon than actually feeding
him with it? Then it's time to start letting him
take over. Load a child-size spoon with a sticky
food that won't slide off, such as oatmeal; put
the spoon in his hand; and guide it to his
mouth. He'll be feeding himself with a utensil
on his own in the second year.

# 218

## spray for fun

Babies love new sensations, and being sprinkled on the tummy with cooling drops of water is a particularly refreshing one. Use a clean squirt bottle to spray your baby with a fine mist of water.

# 219

## count it up

This classic counting rhyme will prime your baby for when she learns numbers later on.

*One, two, buckle my shoe.*
*Three, four, shut the door.*
*Five, six, pick up sticks.*
*Seven, eight, lay them straight.*
*Nine, ten, do it again!*

**6+**

6 months & up

# 220

## greet him on the fly

Next time you're pushing your baby on a playground
bucket swing, enhance the physical fun by cheerfully
saying "bye" when you push the swing up and
reuniting with a happy "hi" when the swing comes
back to you. He may not understand the words, but
he'll notice the repeating sounds, and may kick his
feet in anticipation of the next push of the swing.

# 221

## bathe with buoyancy

Collect assorted floating objects — like waterproof toys
and plastic bottles (tape caps securely shut) — and set
the little flotilla adrift in the bath. Your little sailor will
love watching them bobble and hearing you name
and describe any objects she manages to catch.

# 222

"follow my lead...
My preferences are important,
so when I'm ready to play ball,
I hope you'll be ready to play
ball with me, too!"

# 223

## permit peaceful moments

In the hustle and bustle of life with a baby, it can be difficult to balance work, play, and exercise with quiet time. Try to indulge in peaceful moments with your child – whether you're sitting on the lawn listening to birds sing or just lying on the bed watching the ceiling fan spin around. Quiet time gives you and your baby a chance to relax and bond in a deeper way than when you're rushing between places and activities.

# 224

## look up, up, and away

Point out birds, butterflies, planes, and other winged wonders to your baby to elevate his perspective.

# 225

## make a book

Even at this tender age, babies begin to express their interests. One may be enamoured of ducks, another of trees. Indulge your baby's fancies by making a book about her favourite subject. Punch holes in several pieces of cardboard, string them together with cotton, and stick in pictures from magazines or even your own drawings. As she grows older, this type of book conveys the idea that a single thing can be portrayed in many different ways.

# 226

## spoon it out

Raid the cutlery drawer for large spoons and spatulas that your baby can wave, bang, and lick. Show him how to pass a spoon from hand to hand, which will teach him how to grasp with one hand while releasing with the other – no small feat for a baby.

# 227

## row your boat

Take your baby for a make-believe boat ride to the tune of "Row, Row, Row your Boat". Sit with your knees bent and your feet flat on the floor. Position your little sailor with her back against your tummy. Gently rock forwards and back as you hold her hands and "row" together. The rocking will stimulate her vestibular system (which helps her balance) – and work your abs!

# 228

## sing a highchair song

Belt out this ditty (to the tune of "Shortnin' Bread") whenever you're about to feed your baby — especially if he's a little agitated.

*Sittin' in my highchair, highchair, my chair*
*Sittin' in my highchair, banging my spoon*
*Bring on the jelly, bring on the bread*
*Somebody get this baby fed.*

*Sittin' in my highchair, highchair, my chair*
*Sittin' in my highchair, banging my spoon*
*Bring on the carrots, bring on the peas*
*Somebody feed this baby, please!*

# 229

## meet the animals

You may not be ready to bring
home a pet goldfish, guinea pig,
puppy, or iguana, but your baby
will love seeing the animal world
in action. A well-stocked pet shop
can provide almost as much fun
as a zoo, because babies are as
captivated by a domestic mouse
as they are by an African lion.

# 230

## get wet

If the weather's warm enough, pour a shallow amount
of water into a large bowl or paddling pool outside
and let your baby splash around. Add small plastic
watering cans, buckets, and rubber ducks for more
fun – but never leave her alone, not even for a minute.

# 231

## pull a switcheroo

Stand in front of your baby and hold a small puppet
or soft toy behind your back. Bring it out in front
of you and show it to your baby, using first your left
hand, then your right, then your left again. Soon
you'll be able to tell by his expectant gaze that he's
anticipating which hand will have the toy. Try varying
the pattern you use. Can he anticipate that one, too?

# 232

## make merry music

Music takes on new meaning when your baby learns about making it with other people (not just listening to it). Pick up a recorder or drum; hand her a tambourine or rattle. Even if you're only able to *ting-ting* a triangle, you'll both love the music that you make together.

# 233

## stock up his drawer

At age six months and up, babies develop a pattern: see, grab, and let go. Rather than chastising your curious one for doing what comes naturally, fill a low drawer with items he can explore whenever he wants. Stock toys, cups, unused sponges, or whatever is on hand that's safe and easy for him to handle.

# 234

## expand your storytime talk

Hearing books read aloud is important for all children — even those who are already reading on their own. But reading the printed words isn't enough. Expand your baby's vocabulary and introduce new ideas by talking about what's on the page, such as the various colours and shapes. This type of storytime discussion will engage your child for years to come.

# 235

## kiss with gusto

Babies learn that kissing is a sign of affection, and they start kissing back at about eight months of age. Encourage your little smoocher by asking "Who wants a kiss? Who wants a kiss?" Then make an exaggerated sound as you plant one on her cheek.

# 236

"let me hang out with babies...
Although I can't play with
them yet, I'm fascinated by
other people my size."

# 237

## knock his socks off

It's inevitable: once your baby figures out how to pull off his stretchy little socks and expose his toes, he'll do it repeatedly. This activity gives him a precious sense of self-determination and helps build co-ordination. So go ahead and applaud his efforts. As long as it's not cold, it's okay to bare those tootsies.

# 238

## say "thank you"

Her emerging awareness of social relations means that she'll get a kick out of the simple game of handing you toys and hearing you say "thank you" again and again. Besides entertaining her, this little ritual introduces her to a core concept of etiquette: expressing gratitude.

# 239

## fill up the jar

Once your baby can sit up on his own, give him a plastic jar with an extra-wide mouth and some small, age-appropriate toys. Guide his hand and show him how to put the toys into the jar; this teaches him about spatial relations ("How much stuff fits in here?"). Then demonstrate how to remove the toys, which boosts his problem-solving skills ("How can I get these toys out?").

# 240

## give a juggling lesson

With a toy in each of her hands, what will your baby do if you offer her a third toy? Will she try to grab it with her hands full? Or drop everything? In time, she'll put down one toy before grasping another.

# 241

## try a new peekaboo

You and your baby have probably derived hours of pleasure from playing the classic game of peekaboo, in which you cover and uncover your face with your hands. Try a new version the next time you change your child's nappy: instead of hiding your face, place a clean nappy on your baby's face. When he reaches out to pull it off, help him remove it, and exclaim, "Peekaboo!" This game helps him understand that both you and he still exist even when he's "hiding".

6+

6 months & up

# 242

## teach the sign for "drink"

Babies can learn signs long before they learn to speak, and this early signing is believed to help them acquire spoken language more easily. So teach your baby some signs, such as this one for "drink": curl your hand as if you are holding a cup and bring it to your lips. Make this motion every time you give your baby a drink. Soon she'll do it herself to show you that she's thirsty.

# 243

## phone home

If your baby watches you intently during your phone conversations, let him in on the mystery. The next time you talk to a caller he knows well, put the phone up to his ear so he can hear that familiar voice. Soon he'll be ready to babble some replies.

# 244

## buzz with the bees

Babies love the bee sounds in this rhyme,
especially when they're accompanied
with a little tickling action.

*Here is a beehive.*
make one of your hands into a fist

*Where are the bees?*
make an "I don't know" open-palm
gesture with the other hand

*Hidden away where nobody sees.*
hide your fist behind your back

*Soon they will come,*
*Creeping out from the hive,*
bring your fist in front of you again

*One, two, three, four, five!*
open your fist one finger at a time

*Buzzzzzzzzzz! Buzzzz!*
tickle your baby

6+

6 months & up

# 245

## *make the balls disappear*

Put on a magic show for your baby by rolling some balls
through a cardboard tube. She'll be fascinated as she
watches the balls disappear – then suddenly reappear.
This trick will also teach her about object permanence
(the idea that an object doesn't cease to exist just
because it's not visible) and spatial relations (the way
some things, like balls, fit into other things).

# 246

## present some pasta

Put a spoonful of cool, wet, cooked spaghetti on your baby's highchair tray. He'll enjoy trying to peel apart and squish the slippery strands.

# 247

## feel the fruit

You've just come in, and you need 10 minutes to put away the shopping. So plunk your little one down on the kitchen floor and present some play-worthy produce to engross her, within your field of vision, while you finish your task. She'll love the way the rough-skinned melon and the sweet-smelling oranges roll in funny, unpredictable ways.

# 248

## bend those knees

Even after your baby has mastered the fine art of pulling himself up to a standing position by holding onto the nearest object – be it an armchair or your leg – he may be unsure how to get back down on the floor. You may find his bewildered look adorable at first, but after he's called you again and again, it loses some of its charm. To teach him how to lower himself without falling, gently push behind his knees to make them bend. Then guide him down and slightly forwards until he ends up on his knees. After a few days' practice, he'll be pulling himself up and plopping down with ease.

# 249

## record her voice

As your child starts to understand that she is actually a separate person (a concept that fully develops when she's 12 to 15 months old), hearing her own voice will thrill her. Record her gurgling, babbling, and giggling, then play it back for her. This also will give you an audio scrapbook of some of your baby's first sounds.

# 250

## share a laugh

This is the age when babies start laughing at their own humour. The "joke" may be dropping a toy on the floor, shrieking at passersby, or making open-mouthed faces. Whatever tickles your baby's fancy, let it tickle yours as well. Laughing at his jokes shows him that he has the power to amuse people.

# 251

## find the sheep

This classic nursery rhyme is particularly appealing to babies if you use a toy sheep to act out the story.

*Little Bo-Peep has lost her sheep*
*And doesn't know where to find them.*
*Leave them alone*
*And they'll come home*
*Wagging their tails behind them.*

# 252

## bang away

Set a metal, rimmed baking tray on the floor in front of your baby or on his highchair tray, then give him a selection of hard objects, such as wooden blocks, metal spoons, and plastic cups. Help him drop the objects onto the tray. Which bang does he like best?

253

6+

6 months & up

"let me play with the lights...
On, off, on, off, on, off —
look what I can do!"

# 254

## give her a hand

By six months, many infants are ready to learn to clap.
Gently hold your baby's hands between yours and
clap them together while chanting a nursery rhyme
such as "Patty Cake". Eventually she'll get the hang
of the routine and start clapping on her own.

# 255

## sock it away

Play with your baby's budding understanding of
object permanence (that an object exists even when it
isn't visible) by placing a small toy in an adult-size
sock. Show him how you pull the toy out by reaching
your hand inside the sock. Before you know it, he'll
begin to look in the sock for the missing toy himself.

# 256

## sing a song of teeth

Clean those emerging first teeth and surrounding gums with a wet thin flannel, a piece of gauze, or a baby toothbrush – no need for toothpaste just yet. Introduce this cleaning routine in baby steps: open your own mouth wide to encourage imitation; then start with just one quick, shallow swipe in your baby's mouth. You can get more thorough as the action becomes familiar. Add some fun to the routine by singing this song to the tune of "Here We Go Round the Mulberry Bush":

*This is the way we brush our teeth*
*Brush our teeth*
*Brush our teeth*
*This is the way we brush our teeth*
*So early in the morning!*

# 257

## search for the baby

When you pull a shirt over your child's head,
at the moment her face is hidden by the shirt, ask
enthusiastically, "Where's the baby?" When her face
reappears, say "There she is!" Vary the game by lifting
her over your head while you pretend to search for her,
then bringing her face-to-face for a cheerful reunion.

# 258

## hop for fun

He can't jump, he can't walk, and he may not even be
sitting on his own yet, but your baby will be thrilled to
hop up and down in a jumpy seat — and his legs will get
stronger with each takeoff and landing. Clamp the seat
onto an extra-wide door frame so he has plenty of room
to move around, and stay nearby to ensure his safety.

# 259

## pop open an umbrella

Babies make an easy-to-impress audience. From
your baby's viewpoint, for example, an umbrella
mysteriously transforms — with a click and a swoosh —
from a long, wrinkled object to a smooth, colourful
expanse. So open an umbrella in front of her with a bit
of drama and say: "Open sesame!" followed by a
quick Mary Poppins-style twirl of the umbrella.
You'll win her entertainer-of-the-year award!

# 260

## create a crawl course

Once your child masters the art of crawling,
set up an easy obstacle course where he can
hone his problem-solving abilities and practise
the gross motor skills that his newly acquired
mobility requires. Choose an area with a soft
rug, or roll out a mat or blanket to cushion
his hands and knees. Set up small cushions
and piles of blankets for him to clamber over;
be ready to give him a boost over obstacles if
he needs it. Drape sheets over chairs to create
tunnels to crawl through, and hide toys for
him to discover along the way.

# 261

## drum it up

Hold off on the drum set until your baby is a
teenager – or at least until she can sit up by herself! In
the meantime, let her pound away on other percussive
objects, like saucepans and plastic containers. Early
exploration of sound teaches her about rhythm.

# 262

## lavish him with kisses

By now, your baby is old enough to see the joy in
kisses that depart from the norm. Try an Eskimo kiss
(rubbing noses), a butterfly kiss (fluttering your
eyelashes against his cheek), and an angel kiss
(lightly kissing his eyelids). Before long, he'll be
kissing you back in a variety of ways.

# 263

## *make a splash*

The game of dropsie takes on a whole new meaning when you add water. Partially fill a bath, then give your baby waterproof toys and balls to drop into it. The resulting splash will delight her, and the actions she's performing will develop her hand-eye co-ordination, exercise her grasp-and-release skills, and demonstrate cause and effect. (Always closely supervise water play.)

# 264

## *feast on finger foods*

Once your baby can feed himself, encourage him to practise this skill by laying out bite-sized morsels that you can enjoy together. This allows him to show off his all-important pincer grasp using his forefinger and thumb – and bask in a special meal just with you.

# 265

## describe the world

The more you talk, the more your baby will hear, and the more words she'll store in her memory. Providing a running commentary on everyday life introduces her to the rhythms of speech. Through this, she'll begin to understand the world around her and how people explain things to each other. One day you'll hear her telling her teddy something in the same tone you used to explain it to her – and you'll know she was listening.

# 266

## go bottoms-up

Lie on your back, with knees bent and feet flat on the floor, and lay your baby on your shins, facing you. Holding him snugly, curl your knees towards your nose until he's horizontal or tip him slightly bottoms-up.

# 9+

## nine months & up

At this age, even those babies who aren't yet walking are beginning to look and act like toddlers. Games that allow your child to practise gross motor skills – crawling, pulling himself up to stand, cruising across the floor, or climbing – are particularly appealing to him now because mobility is his main objective. Fine motor skills are also important to him. He may insist on turning the pages of a book or stacking bricks on his own. Get ready: this is the beginning of the do-it-myself stage.

# 267

## play peekaboo with toys

Reinforce the concept of object permanence (the idea that objects exist even when they aren't visible) by making a big show of hiding a toy under a blanket and then helping your child find it. Soon she'll learn to recognize shapes by the hidden toy's outline – for instance, the telltale lump of her toy bunny. If she's having trouble finding the toy, cover just part of it.

# 268

## pull out a laundry basket

Chances are you already own one of the world's most versatile baby toys: the laundry basket. It makes a perfect fort, playpen, or doll cot. Your baby can also throw toys in it and push it around, or climb in and get you to pull him across the floor. One day you may even get to put laundry in the basket again!

# 269

## hop to it

You can stimulate your child's sense of balance using a large vinyl "hopping" ball with a handle (sold at toy shops and sporting-goods shops). Although her feet can't yet touch the ground when she's on the ball, let her hold the handle. Bounce the ball gently with one hand, keeping her upright with the other.

# 270

## play hide-and-seek

After months of experimenting with the concept of object permanence (the notion that objects exist even when they aren't visible), your baby is finally ready for the big time: a game of hide-and-seek, where both baby and grown-up get to do the hiding and the seeking. But don't do a really good job of hiding, because that might frustrate or scare your baby. Instead, help him by calling out, "Come and find me! Where am I?" This game isn't just fun for babies – it also helps them work through separation anxiety as they see you "return" after your "disappearances".

# 271

## master the stairs

Although it's tempting to turn stairs into a forbidden zone, it's better to teach your baby how to navigate them safely. Climbing up doesn't take much practice, but to go down safely, she needs to turn onto her front and lower her feet down onto each step below her. Once she learns how to feel for a solid object behind her feet, she'll have the foundation not only for stair-climbing but also for later pursuits, such as scrambling around a play structure as a pre-schooler or scaling rocks as a teenager. Always make sure the stairs' safety gates are securely closed when your baby is not practising her climbing under your supervision.

# 272

## introduce push toys

Even before he masters alternating his legs to propel himself on a riding toy, your child can push himself with both legs at once. This pushing action allows him to strengthen his muscles and experience the joy of independent mobility. Stay nearby, as your baby may still need a helping hand to keep him balanced and safe.

# 273

## bring out the brushes

Water play in all forms will be a hit for years to come with your little one. On a warm afternoon, give her some cheap paintbrushes and a bucket of water, and let her "paint" the pavement.

**9+**

9 months & up

# 274

## get out the muffin tray

Once your baby has mastered the ability to pick up
and release objects, he'll enjoy plopping tennis balls,
toys, and wads of crumpled-up paper into the cups of
muffin trays – an action that hones fine motor skills.

# 275

## stuff a box

Cut a large hole in the lid or side of a shoe box, then
show your baby how to stuff toys through the hole and
into the box. She'll learn about the relative sizes
of toys and about object permanence (the fact that an
object still exists even when it's not visible). Picking
up and pushing toys through the hole will also help
her develop her fine motor skills, as will sticking her
hand into the hole to take the toys out again.

# 276

## smell intriguing scents

Gather some small plastic containers, such as film canisters, and look in your kitchen cupboards for some strongly scented ingredients to insert inside each container. For example, saturate a cotton wool ball with vanilla extract. Put one ingredient into each container, close and tape it securely shut, then poke holes in the lid. Let your baby sniff the scents.

# 277

## steer a baby wheelbarrow

This activity strengthens your child's upper body and develops his co-ordination: pick him up by his hips or under his chest so he can "walk" on his hands. When he's older and stronger, hold up his feet instead.

**9+**

9 months & up

# 278

## visit the zoo

If your baby crows over animals seen in the distance and in books and has enjoyed visits to pet shops, seek opportunities for her to see new species and perhaps even touch some live critters. Visit a children's zoo to introduce her to the amazing creatures that inhabit our planet. Be sure to supervise your little one's interspecies meeting, and wash her hands afterwards.

# 279

## give him a lift

Let your child experience the joy of motion with this
up-in-the-air game. Sit on a carpeted floor with your
baby facing you. Lift him up and, while holding him
firmly, roll back so that he "flies" over your head. This
action strengthens his back and stimulates the
vestibular system, which helps him balance. It's also
likely to prompt a lot of giggles from your copilot.

# 280

## soar down the slide

At first, your baby may want to go down the kiddie
slide only with your help — guiding her from the side
and catching her at the end. Over time, however, as
she feels safer, she'll want to whiz down all by herself.

# 281

## sort the shapes

With a shape-sorter toy, first show your child how the round piece fits into the round hole, then show him how the square and triangular pieces fit into their matching holes. Soon he'll be matching up the shapes himself. This activity teaches spatial relations and shape discrimination, and develops fine motor skills.

# 282

## encourage early walkers

The primary challenge of walking is finding one's balance. To help your toddler-to-be get up — and stay up — give her objects that provide resistance and stability but are light enough for her to push. A laundry basket filled with clothes works well. Avoid baby walkers and tricycles, however, as they roll too quickly.

# 283

"watch home movies with me...
I like to see all the fascinating
people — especially Mummy
and Daddy — and that cute
baby doing fun things. "

# 284

## teach the concept of size

Your baby will enjoy trying to imitate you as
you do the hand gestures of this simple rhyme.

*Big fish, little dish*
hold your hands out wide, then cup them together

*Big log, little dog*
hold your hands out wide, then close them together

*Big rug, little bug*
stretch your arms out, then put your index
fingers and thumbs close together

*Big sky, little guy*
open your arms up wide, then hug your baby

# 285

## construct a cardboard house

An older baby's love of child-sized spaces, the peekaboo game, and imitative play means that he'll be thrilled to have his own house – be it ever so humble. Get a big box from an appliance store, cut out windows and a door, and decorate the exterior with paint and stickers. Tuck blankets and toys inside to create a cosy retreat for the new tenant.

# 286
## draw together

It will be a few years before your baby can draw anything even remotely resembling, well, anything. Still, she'll enjoy drawing lines with a crayon, marker, or piece of chalk. If she can't do it herself, hold her hand gently in yours and guide it on the paper.

# 287
## bedazzle with balloons

When your baby tugs on the strings of helium-filled balloons, he'll be greatly intrigued at how his movements make the balloons bounce all around. Choose foil balloons; unlike latex ones, they don't pop, so they're less likely to be ingested. Always supervise balloon play and make sure that the strings are short so your baby doesn't get tangled in them.

# 288

## give encouragement

Praise – in the form of "You're such a good girl!"
or "What a smart girl!" – generally focusses on the
child herself. Encouragement, on the other hand,
is aimed at a child's efforts: "You really worked hard
to get up that hill!" or "I'm amazed at how fast you
can run!" Most experts agree that encouraging a
child is preferable to praising her, because praise
sets the child up for wanting to always be "smart",
"good", or "strong", whereas encouragement
focuses on the child's actions and not her worth
as a person. Start boosting your baby's sense
of competence now, as she's becoming aware of
herself as a separate being who needs to be
recognized as both lovable and capable.

# 289

## get tools for tots

Older babies and toddlers are keenly interested in imitating the grown-ups in their lives, so you may find your little one trying to brush his own hair, sweep up crumbs, or bang a hammer. Keep him safe yet satisfied by giving him toy versions of the tools you use around the house. Whether he's fiddling in a play kitchen or pottering in a pretend workshop, this initial imitating behaviour will evolve into fully-fledged fantasy play later on, in which armchairs serve as pirate ships and leaves are ingredients for a magic potion.

# 290

## stack the rings

Your child won't be able to stack coloured rings on
a plastic toy pole in order from large to small until
she's closer to two years old. At this stage, urge her to
use her budding problem-solving skills and hand-eye
co-ordination to stack the rings in any order – and to
enjoy what she does best now: take things apart!

# 291

## cut to the chase

Whether he's waddling around on two feet or
zipping around on all fours, your baby will love
an active game of chase. Keep it gentle – you don't
want to frighten him – but motivate him with words of
encouragement, funny noises, and lots of laughter.
Then change it around so he gets to chase you, too.

# 292

## burst the bubbles

Your baby has always loved to watch you blow soap bubbles, and at about nine months of age, she's now ready to reach out and pop them. So encourage her! She'll practise her hand-eye co-ordination – and she will feel proud of her popping performance.

# 293

## dial his number

Fascinated by the ringing and all the buttons, your baby may already be grabbing for your phone. End the power struggle by giving him one of his own. Whether it's a toy or an unwanted cordless phone, pretending to use it will make him feel like Mummy or Daddy. At the same time, he'll get to practise his language and social skills.

# 294

## talk into a tube

If your child is intrigued by sounds – especially the funny ones she makes herself – then talking (or rather, babbling) through a tube might be a lot of fun for her. Pick up a kitchen-paper or wrapping-paper tube and show her how to talk, blow, hum, and sing through it. Then let her take a turn.

# 295

## give him a rucksack

When he sees an older sibling – or a carer – using a rucksack, your little one will probably want to have one, too. Although he can't wear a sack until he's a steady walker, he'll enjoy helping you fill his personal sack with toys, snacks, or books – and then dumping them out again.

9+

9 months & up

# 296

"show me how to drop balls...
It teaches me to aim and let
go – and it makes a great sound,
especially when it lands in
a big bowl of water!"

# 297

## take turns

Your child will jump at the chance to practise walking by pulling or pushing a sturdy truck. Take turns with her: first give her a ride in the truck, then have her give her small charges (dolls and soft toys) a ride.

# 298

## challenge his balancing skills

Kids love to test their balancing skills by trying to crawl or walk along wide beams in parks and at children's play centres. They can enjoy such balancing acts at home, too: simply lean a broad, firm board up against a low, sturdy chair or table. Make sure the floor underneath is cushioned. Then, as you stand beside him or hold his hand, encourage him to crawl or walk up and down the board.

# 299

## play jack-in-the-box

This old-fashioned toy, with its tinkling tune and pop-up puppet, continues to delight children, even the very young. Help your baby turn the handle and stuff the puppet back into the box after it pops up – but no one needs to teach her how to laugh when that puppet magically greets her again and again!

# 300

## wrap him up

Unroll about 120 cm (4 ft) of wrapping paper on the floor and plop your baby in the middle of it. He'll enjoy rolling on it, tearing it, crackling it, and pulling it across his body. Just make sure he doesn't tear off any pieces and put them in his mouth, as they could pose a choking hazard.

# 301

## bathe the toy babies

Set up a small bath with warm water and soap suds to give your baby a chance to bathe her own "babies", whether they're dolls, rubber ducks, or plastic dinosaurs. Remember to supervise her at all times, and keep a towel on hand for spills.

# 302

## take a dip

And he thought his little bath was fun! From the safety of your arms, your little swimmer can learn to feel comfortable in the wide-open space of a pool. Bounce through the water together while he revels in the sensation of weightlessness and discovers the joy of kicking and splashing. (Never leave your child unattended in or near a pool.)

# 303

## get cheeky

In the realm of simple baby pleasures, squashing a parent's puffed-out cheeks between two hands ranks highly, especially if you act very surprised each time your baby does it.

# 304

## pour another one

Your baby sees you pouring liquids all day long: a cup of coffee for yourself, some milk into her bottle, or water into the cat's bowl. From her perspective, this looks like a lot of fun. So give her a turn: when she's in the bath, let her practise pouring with plastic cups and bottles. She'll develop an awareness of size and volume while sharpening her fine motor skills.

# 305

## *explore the world on foot*

If your baby's walking, provide him with plenty of
opportunities to amble down the pavement, meander
along a dirt path, or waddle across a grassy lawn.
He sharpens his powers of observation as he picks
up stones and sticks, listens to his shoes tapping on
the concrete, and stops to examine scurrying bugs.

# 306

## give puppet kisses

Don a small hand puppet and use it to give "kisses"
to different parts of your baby's body. She'll love to hear
you tell her where the puppet is going to kiss her next.

# 307

## sing for your supper

Make mealtime even more fun for your wee one by
reciting this time-honoured rhyme as he enjoys his food.

*Sippity sup, sippity sup,*
*Bread and milk from a china cup.*
*Bread and milk from a bright silver spoon,*
*Made of a piece of the bright silver moon.*
*Sippity sup, sippity sup,*
*Sippity, sippity, sup!*

# 308

## wave bye-bye

Saying good-bye is one of the first social rituals babies learn because it's a gesture they can easily recognize and copy. By teaching your child about language ("bye-bye!") and routines (the action of waving every time someone leaves), you establish a soothing ritual that might help her if separation anxiety is making departures difficult.

# 309

## play ball

Balls are an all-time favourite toy. Give your child a variety of different-sized balls and notice how he adapts his play for each one. Demonstrate the possibilities: throwing, rolling, bouncing, catching.

**9+**

9 months & up

# 310

## sing "where is thumbkin?"

Borrowing the melody of "Frère Jacques" and adding some peekaboo fun, this fingerplay will amuse your baby well into her pre-school years. Start with both your fists behind your back.

*Where is Thumbkin? Where is Thumbkin?*
*Here I am.*
bring your right hand out with your thumb up

*Here I am.*
bring your left hand out with your thumb up

*How are you today, sir?*
bend your right thumb as if talking

*Very well, I thank you.*
bend your left thumb as if talking

*Run away.*
put your right hand behind your back

*Run away.*
put your left hand behind your back

continue with "Pointer", "Middle Finger", "Ring Finger", and "Pinkie"

# 311

## let 'er rip!

Before you toss out your monthly magazines, hand one or two to your baby to explore something different: the thrill of tearing out the pages! The ripping action sounds great and helps him develop both gross and fine motor skills. Watch him closely to make sure he doesn't put any paper in his mouth.

# 312

## broaden your circle

Schedule get-togethers with other parents and babies. Even though your baby won't play with other children until she's near the end of her second year, she'll enjoy watching and imitating them. And you'll learn from observing other babies – and parents, too!

9+

9 months & up

# 313

## reverse the roles

At about nine months, babies start imitating the
grown-ups and older kids in their lives and enjoy
giving them some personal attention. So encourage
your child to put food in your mouth, dab your face
with a flannel, and brush your hair. It makes
him feel like a big person and allows him to be
the nurturer, not just the one being nurtured.

# 314

## give her a foot rub

Feet are wonderfully sensitive to touch. Treat your
active baby to a relaxing foot massage before she goes
to bed. Softly rub the bottom of each toe, then make
circular movements on her heels with your thumbs.
For a more soothing massage, use a baby lotion.

# 315

"show me creepy crawlies...
I like to watch worms wiggle
around, big bugs crawl up and
down, and ants run all around."

9+

9 months & up

# 316

## play at the beach

With plenty of sun protection and supervision, the beach makes a wonderful destination for you and your baby. He can dig in the sand, slap the water, watch the birds, and go for a dip – in an adult's arms, of course.

# 317

## point out the body parts

Share this classic children's song with your baby by demonstrating the movements as you sing. Then repeat the song and help her focus on her own body parts by guiding her hands to the appropriate places.

*Head, shoulders, knees, and toes*
touch your hands to these body parts in order

*Knees and toes!*
pat your knees and toes

*Head, shoulders, knees, and toes*
touch your hands to these body parts in order

*Knees and toes!*
pat your knees and toes

*Eyes and ears and mouth and nose*
touch your hands to these body parts in order

*Head, shoulders, knees, and toes*
touch your hands to these body parts in order

*Knees and toes!*
pat your knees and toes

9+

9 months & up

# 318

## puzzle it out

Exercise your baby's spatial-relation and fine motor skills with durable wooden puzzles. Start with a basic circle-shaped puzzle with only one piece; once he masters that, graduate to a puzzle with a few more pieces. Look for easy-to-grasp knobs, bright colours, and matching pictures or patterns on the board that will help him determine where each piece goes. Show him how to slide the pieces into place.

# 319

## hide the toy

Tie a long ribbon onto a favourite small toy, then let your baby watch as you hide the tethered plaything under the sofa. Help her pull the ribbon to bring the toy back into view. Can she retrieve the toy by herself?

# 320

## elaborate on his past

Talking about what has happened in the past
helps build your baby's capacity to remember.
But don't just talk about common occurrences
or ask questions with "yes" or "no" responses,
such as "Did you have a yummy snack today?"
Instead, elaborate on activities and relationships.
For example, each day, talk about what you did
together, where you went, and the people you saw:
"When we played with your friend Carter at the
park, a big black dog licked your toes!" In time,
as you repeat the more memorable stories, your
child will begin to build what psychologists
call an "autobiographical memory".

# 321

## stack the containers

Show your baby how to balance different-sized plastic containers on top of each other, and how to nest the small containers inside the big ones. This activity teaches spatial relations and how to discriminate between various shapes and sizes. Remember, she'll knock things down before she learns to stack them.

# 322

## give blanket rides

A blanket ride is much like a sledge ride, except that you pull a blanket across a floor or grass instead of a sledge across snow. Sit or lay your child on a blanket, then gently pull the blanket. Try different directions. If you add an older child to the mix, he can ensure that the baby doesn't topple over, plus this doubles the fun!

# 323

## shuffle the magic cups

A slower, simpler version of the classic shell game can be challenging and fun for babies. Show your child that you're putting a small toy or ball under a plastic cup. Then turn over a second cup. Slowly move the cups around. Now ask her to find the toy. She may not get it right away, but if you move the cups very slowly, eventually your baby will be able to guess correctly. (You might try playing with only one cup first to help her understand the game.) This activity will strengthen her visual tracking abilities and expand her powers of concentration.

# 324
## read it one more time

Familiarity breeds contentment in babies, even if the same old same old gets a little, well, old for grown-ups. Try to stay cheerful even if you've read that board book about trains 101 times in the last two weeks. The repetition helps your baby associate words with pictures, an essential step in developing both language and reading skills. And knowing what's coming on the next page makes him feel secure.

# 325
## show her yellow

As your child learns to sort objects by characteristics, colour becomes increasingly important. Try having a yellow day: point out all the yellow objects you see. Green, orange, and purple days are sure to follow.

# 326

## stack the stones

Everyday objects often make the best toys, and a favourite among many babies is a simple pile of dirt-free stones. They're fun to stack, push over, and hit together. Choose lightweight, medium-sized stones that won't pose a choking hazard.

# 327

## teach him rhythm

Research shows that babies can perceive rhythms and anticipate what comes next in a pattern, even if they can't always replicate that pattern. Try this yourself by demonstrating a simple rhythm, like clap-clap-rest, clap-clap-rest. Watch as your baby tries to imitate this rhythm. Pattern recognition is key for learning to talk, read, do maths, and appreciate music.

# 328

"roll the ball to me...
I can stop it with my hands,
and that helps me get more
co-ordinated — and ready for
playing with a friend one day."

# 329

## quack like a duck

Animal sounds, hand gestures, and one bossy
duckling make this song a sure winner.

*Six little ducks that I once knew,*
hold up six fingers

*Fat ones, skinny ones, fair ones, too.*
make hand motions for "fat" and "skinny"

*But the one little duck*
hold up one finger

*With the feather on his back,*
wiggle your fingers near your back

*He led the others*
"walk" fingers of one hand across the palm of the other

*With a "quack, quack, quack",*
open and close your hand like a duck bill

*a "quack, quack, quack".*
open and close your hand like a duck bill

*He led the others with a "quack, quack, quack".*
open and close your hand like a duck bill

# 330

## take the route less travelled

An obstacle course can help your toddler develop balance and foot-eye co-ordination. Arrange small blocks or a broom handle to crawl or step over, hula hoops to go in and out of, a skipping rope laid out in a wavy pattern to follow, and cushions to clamber over. Give her a hand if she needs one: the point is to help her develop as a walker, not to test her.

# 331

## ride a rocking horse

Your little cowboy will love rocking himself back and forth on a plastic pony or classic wooden steed. Set the horse on thick carpet or grass and always stand by, just in case the bronco bucks.

# 332

## rearrange the furniture

The cruising phase – when babies hang on to furniture or human legs for support as they shuffle from one spot to another – is crucial in learning to walk, as it gives babies a chance to practise taking steps. Help your child cruise by creating a chain of sturdy furniture that runs from one side of the room to the other. Move fragile objects, such as lamps, wobbly end tables, or plant stands, away from her eager grasp. This may make your room look a little odd, but most babies go through the cruising stage relatively quickly. And her glee at being able to get around on her own two feet will make the decorating disruption worth it.

9+

9 months & up

# 333

## visit a museum

He can't appreciate the dawn of perspective during the Renaissance, or the odd things that happened to human figures during the Cubist period, but your inquisitive child will still marvel at the colours and forms on display in an art museum. And the halls between galleries are a great place for him to practise his early walking skills. Try to avoid peak hours — and break up the art tour with visits to a café and the outdoors so he doesn't get bored or over-stimulated.

# 334

## revel in quiet reading

Reading to your little one is crucial for developing her love of books. And if she is showing even the slightest interest in looking at books alone, let her enjoy them on her own. It shows that she can entertain herself and that her attention span is increasing.

# 335

## enjoy the magic of magnets

Place a variety of large colourful magnets on the bottom portion of your refrigerator door or on a magnetic board. Help your child experiment with sliding them around, peeling them off, putting them back on, and sticking them together. (Avoid small magnets that can pose a choking hazard.)

# 336

## sing the colour song

Help your baby learn about basic colours by singing
this song as you point out examples of each colour,
like the red sock, the green ball, and the very blue fish.

*Red and orange, green and blue*
*Shiny yellow and pink, too.*
*I love colours, and I love you!*

# 337

## record a book on tape

When you leave your child with a babysitter, ease his
separation anxiety by recording yourself reading one
of his favourite books. He'll love hearing your voice
when you're not there, and listening to the familiar
words will comfort him. For nap time, record several
books in a row for him to listen to as he falls asleep.

# 338

## wrap old favourites

Your baby might enjoy seeing some old friends. If you loosely wrap a few of her favourite toys in wrapping paper, her play can start with crinkling the paper and ripping it open. (Just don't let it become a snack!)

# 339

## climb the ladder

Crawling and climbing are similar cross-lateral movements – one is horizontal and the other vertical. Show your baby how to move his hands and feet up the rungs of a ladder, such as the one on a slide. Stand behind and below him, and guide him the whole way. Soon he'll be clambering up the ladder all by himself.

# 340

## enjoy a knee ride

Seat your baby on your knees facing you, then hold
her securely for this gentle but bouncy ride.

*Down by the banks of the Hanky Panky*
gently bounce your baby up and down on your knees

*Where the bullfrogs jump from bank to banky*
lift your baby onto one knee, then onto the other knee

*With a hip, hop, hippity hop*
gently bounce your baby up and down on your knees

*Jump off the lily pad, and kerplop!*
while holding your baby securely, gently
lean her backwards as if she's falling

# 341

## invite the toys to tea

Once your baby learns the purpose of using a cup,
demonstrate how to give his teddy bear or doll an
occasional "sip" of his water or (pretend) tea. He may
laugh or even copy this bit of make-believe – a small
precursor of all the imaginative play ahead.

# 342

## water the plants together

Your baby loves to imitate you, and she's fascinated
with water. So what better way to amuse her than
by letting her water some outdoor plants? Hold her
hands on a watering can or – for even more fun – use
a hose. Of course, most of the water will go on her feet
(and yours) and not on the plants, but she'll enjoy
feeling like a big person – and getting a bit wet!

**9+**

9 months & up

# 343

## walk tall

Congratulate your aspiring little walker with this charming song about one of life's most amazing milestones. Sing it to the tune of "I'm a Little Teapot".

*I'm a little walker, I walk tall.*
*Sometimes I stumble, sometimes I fall.*
*But now I'm two-legged, so hear me call:*
*"I'm walking tall and having a ball!"*

# 344

## bring out old-timers

Even though your baby has outgrown his infant toys, the rattles can delight him in new, exciting ways. Make a game by hiding them in a shoe box, assembling a rattle "band", or stacking them up.

# 345

"dance with me...
I may rock, sway, or just nod
my head, but however I
dance, I'll learn about rhythm
and self-expression."

9+

9 months & up

# 346

## give her an earful

Long loved as a camp and hiking chant, "Do Your Ears Hang Low?", with its accompanying hand motions, can also entertain infants who are learning about ears.

*Do your ears hang low?*
tug on your earlobes

*Do they wobble to and fro?*
quickly wiggle your earlobes

*Can you tie them in a knot?*
mime tying a knot

*Can you tie them in a bow?*
mime tying a bow

*Can you throw them o'er your shoulder*
mime throwing something over your shoulder

*Like a Continental soldier?*
salute and march in place

*Do your ears hang low?*
tug on your earlobes

# 347

## teach "simon says"

Your baby's too young to play this game by the rules of the playground set. But a simplified version will teach him to listen to verbal directions and organize his body in order to follow them. Use simple commands at first, such as "Simon says touch your toes" or "Simon says open your mouth". Always demonstrate what you want your baby to do so he can try to imitate you.

# 348

## grab for gadgets

Your baby is at the peak age for seeking out everyday objects, such as cups, plastic hangers, and boxes. These simple household items are just as effective as top-of-the-line developmental toys for practising her fine motor skills and indulging in imitative play.

9+

9 months & up

# 349

## build a sandcastle

He'll need help making the basic structure, but your young architect can pack a pail full of sand all by himself or just pile on handfuls of the stuff. The tactile stimulation of sand is irresistible, and the teamwork sets the foundation for future co-operative play.

# 350

## run interference

Can't keep your baby from reaching into the rubbish bin or unrolling the toilet paper? You say "no" again and again, but temptation still gets the better of her. Try saying "no" to the undesired behaviour just once or twice, then distract her with something equally intriguing. If she's digging in the rubbish, for instance, hand her a basket of toys to search through.

# 351

## say "good night"

To ease bedtime transitions, walk around the house with your baby saying good night to familiar objects: "Good night, teddy bear. Good night, sofa. Good night, toothbrush. Good night, Mummy's bed," and so on. This creates a soothing ritual for your baby and helps expand his vocabulary.

# 352

## touch and talk

Help your baby develop tactile awareness. Fill a large, wide-mouthed plastic jar with items that have a very distinctive feel, like a soft toy dog, a plastic fish, and a rubber ball. As your baby enjoys pulling each object out of the jar, talk about what she's touching: "This dog is so soft!" and "Does that fish feel funny?"

**9+**

9 months & up

# 353

## meet the animals

Older babies, who are intrigued by the sounds
and adventures of animals, get a kick out of
"The Animal Fair" — especially if you sing the
song on the way to the zoo or circus.

*I went to the Animal Fair.*
*The birds and the beasts were there.*
*The big baboon by the light of the moon*
*Was combing his auburn hair.*

*You should have seen the monk.*
*He sat on the elephant's trunk.*
*The elephant sneezed and fell on his knees*
*And that was the end of the monk,*
*The monk, the monk, the monk.*

# 354

## play with pretend food

Given your baby's emerging interest in imaginative play and his budding ability to feed himself, try having a pretend meal with him, using plastic food and cutlery. Choose large pieces of "food" that don't pose a choking hazard.

# 355

## pedal away

When your baby reaches her first year, she's ready for the thrill of joining you on a bicycle ride – as long as she's wearing a helmet and sitting snugly in an approved child's seat or trailer. Travel on cycle paths or well-paved roads with minimal traffic, and stop often to talk about the sights – and to check on her.

# 356

## flip some lids

Let your baby practise his manual-dexterity skills on a couple of large plastic storage jars with screw-top lids. Start by just resting a lid on top of a jar. Show him how to screw the lid on and off, and then let him try it.

# 357

## do broom pull-ups

To strengthen your baby's hands, arms, upper torso, and back, hold a broomstick horizontally in front of her, get her to grasp the stick with both hands, then slowly lift her a few centimetres off the ground (so she doesn't fall far if she lets go). At first she may not be able to hold on, but after some practice your little gymnast may be able to suspend herself at least partially. Do this exercise over a soft surface, such as a large floor pillow.

# 358

## play a silly name game

Although they can't yet talk and have probably
never seen a stand-up comic (except for you!),
babies nine months and older can understand
silly-sounding words or phrases or even a good
joke – especially if the joke's about them.

*Is your name Muffin Head?*
put your hands on your head

*Is your name Mr. Ed?*
turn your palms upwards and shrug your shoulders

*Is your name Doodlee Doodlee Doo?*
tickle your baby's tummy

*Is your name Bug-a-Boo?*
"walk" your fingers up your baby's chest like a bug

*Is your name (say your baby's name)?*
turn your palms upwards and shrug your shoulders

*It is?*
wave your hands in the air excitedly

*Hurrah!*
clap your hands

# 359

## remember the first words

Whether he says "aye" for hi, "oggo" for go, or "ope"
for toast, make a list – or even a recording on tape or
CD – of your baby's first words. It will bring back
sweet memories for you and your family in later
years – and delight him when he's older, too!

# 360

## massage her head

When your little one is in a quiet mood, pamper her
with a head massage. Gently stroke her face along
the bridge of her nose, then across her brows to her
temples. Next, stroke from her nose across her cheeks.
Finish by massaging along the sides of her face,
including her ears, and finally the back of her head.
Repeat this if she's enjoying your tender touch.

# 361

## pair up the shoes

Turn that jumble of shoes in your hallway or wardrobe into a learning experience. Hand one shoe to your baby and ask him to help you find its mate. Start with one pair; as your baby masters the game, add more.

# 362

## introduce the talking heads

Puppet shows can be an effective tool for demonstrating how conversations work, whether they are between a puppet and your baby or among the puppets themselves – or both. These shows can also model appropriate expressions of emotions. As your child gets older, she may want to speak through the puppets and have them say things she'd be afraid to say herself. Encourage the dialogue.

**9+**

9 months & up

# 363

## go, speed racer

Lean a board or piece of cardboard against a chair or stair. Demonstrate for your baby how fast his wheeled toys can go down the ramp. Then it's his turn.

# 364

## create a messy masterpiece

Provide your petite Picasso with the ingredients to make an artwork: place a pile of whipped cream on her highchair tray, then add a drop or two of food colouring. Show her how fun it is to swirl and smear the whipped cream with her hands all over the tray! Pull out the camera to document her performance art.

# 365

## plan a picnic

Warm sun, happy butterflies, chirping birds,
a soft blanket, and delicious snacks — frankly,
even the ants will enchant your baby at a picnic.
The cuisine may not be sophisticated, but it's the
company (you!) and the fresh air that count.

**9+**

# index
## a, b, c

## about gymboree

Since 1976, Gymboree has helped parents and children discover the many pleasures and benefits of play. Based on established principles of early childhood education and administered by trained teachers, Gymboree Play & Music classes emphasize the wonder of play in a non-competitive, nurturing environment. Gymboree, which runs its interactive parent-child programmes in more than 27 countries, has contributed to the international awareness of the importance of play.

## consultant editors

Dr. Roni Cohen Leiderman is a developmental psychologist specializing in emotional development, positive discipline, and play. For more than 25 years, she has worked with children, families, and professionals. She is associate dean of the Mailman Segal Institute for Early Childhood Studies at Nova Southeastern University in Fort Lauderdale, Florida, and the mother of two children.

Dr. Wendy Masi is a developmental psychologist specializing in early childhood. She has designed and implemented programmes for pre-schools, families with young children, and early childhood professionals for more than 25 years. The mother of four children, Dr. Masi is dean of the Mailman Segal Institute for Early Childhood Studies at Nova Southeastern University.

## author

Susan Elisabeth Davis, the mother of two children and an award-winning journalist, is the author of Gymboree's *Baby Play* and coauthor of Gymboree's *Toddler Play*.

## illustrator

Christine Coirault, a children's book illustrator based in London, is the illustrator of *How Do I Say That?* and the author of *The Little Book of Good Manners*.

## photographer

Aaron Locke, owner of Aaron Locke Design & Photography, specializes in visual storytelling through graphic design and photography services.